James Kig...
Roger Walls...

Colour illustrations by Bob Pearson

The Supermarine Walrus & Stranraer

STRATUS

Published in Poland in 2004 by STRATUS
Artur Juszczak, Po. Box 123, 27-600 Sandomierz 1, Poland
e-mail: arturj@mmpbooks.biz
for
Mushroom Model Publications,
36 Ver Road, Redbourn,
AL3 7PE, UK.
e-mail: rogerw@waitrose.com

© 2004 Mushroom Model Publications.
http://www.mmpbooks.biz

All rights reserved. Apart from any fair dealing for the purpose of private study, research, criticism or review, as permitted under the Copyright, Design and Patents Act, 1988, no part of this publication may be reproduced, stored in a retrieval system, or transmitted in any form or by any means, electronic, electrical, chemical, mechanical, optical, photocopying, recording or otherwise, without prior written permission. All enquiries should be addressed to the publisher.

ISBN 83-917178-9-5

Editor in chief	Roger Wallsgrove
Editorial Team	Bartłomiej Belcarz
	Robert Pęczkowski
	Artur Juszczak
Proofreading	Roger Wallsgrove
Colour Drawings	Bob Pearson
Scale plans	Przemysław Frask
	Mariusz Kubryn

Get in the picture!
Do you have photographs of historical aircraft, airfields in action, or original and unusual stories to tell? MMP would like to hear from you! We welcome previously unpublished material that will help to make MMP books the best of their kind. We will return original photos to you and provide full credit for your images. Contact us before sending us any valuable material: *rogerw@waitrose.com*

Printed by: Drukarnia Diecezjalna, ul. Żeromskiego 4, 27-600 Sandomierz
tel. (15) 832 31 92; fax (15) 832 77 87
www.wds.pl   marketing@wds.pl

WYPRODUKOWANO W POLSCE
PRINTED IN POLAND

On the title page: Walrus I L2228, 700 Sqn., from HMS Sheffield. This aircraft was used for spotting at the battle in Operation 'Collar', an attempt to bring the Italian Navy to battle, by crew Capt J.R.W. Groves, Lt Cdr G Fenwick and Leading Airman Pike, thus acquiting the name "Spotter of Spartivento" on the starboard nose. See pages 13 and 28 for other pictures of this aircraft. (IWM A4055)

Table of contents

Acknowledgements 4
Author's note 5
Introduction 6
Development of Supermarine's single engined seaplanes 8
The Supermarine Seagull V and Walrus 10
Walrus survivors 18
Progeny 22
Walrus Mark Indentification 24
    Seagull V Prototype 24
    Seagull V 26
    Walrus Mk. I 27
    Walrus Mk. II 30
    Technical Details 31
Supermarines's Flying Boats 33
Stranraer 35
    Technical Details 38
Select Bibliography 40
Detail photos 41
    Walrus-Fuselage 41
    Walrus-Exterior 44
    Walrus-Wing 52
    Walrus-Tail 57
    Walrus-Stores 60
    Walrus-Cockpit 63
    Walrus-Interior 71
    Walrus-Engine 75
    Walrus-Floats & Undercarriage 79
    Stranraer-Fuselage 83
    Stranraer-Wings 92
    Stranraer-Tail 97
    Stranraer-Cockpit 99
    Stranraer-Interior 102
Colour Profiles 105

Sole surviving Stranraer CF-BXO looking somewhat neglected and missing the port engine after its use in civilian hands was over and before coming to the RAF Museum. (CanAv)

Development

Acknowledgements

We would like to thank the staff and restoration team at RAAF Point Cook, Victoria, Australia - Ron Gretton, Teena Cardillo, Brad Owen, David Crotty and David Gardner for providing access to and information about their magnificent restoration of Walrus HD874. Likewise the Australian War Memorial were very kind in helping to fill a number of gaps in our pictorial coverage. In the UK, Dick Melton, owner of Walrus G-RNLI, was a fund of anecdotes and Walrus lore, and it was a privilege to be able to see and assess his restoration. Andy Simpson at the RAF Museum provided us with his excellent help to get best possible access to their unique Seagull V and their also unique Stranraer, as well as his detailed history of each machine. Jerry Shore at the FAA Museum provided comprehensive help and insisted we come back for more. In Canada, Christine Dunphy at the Shearwater Aviation Museum provided us with a phenomenal range of Stranraer pictures for use, and Fiona Smith-Hale and Andrew MacDonald at the Canadian Aviation Museum in Rockliffe, Ontario provided, likewise, an excellent collection. Mr Jerry Vernon in B.C., Canada, shared his unrivalled knowledge and contacts on the Stranraer in Canada, and Gordon Parker of WhiskeyJack Decals provided us with several further insights into both the Walrus and the Stranraer. We can state that the book is all the better for this varied and selfless range of contributions. Further information was provided by Steve Atkin on G-RNLI, Peter Eliott and Darran Cowd at the RAF Museum, the Public Record Office at Kew, and Dave Parry at the Imperial War Museum photo archive. A special thanks goes to Jo Mitchell who provided copies of A.E. Mitchell's photographs of the prototype Seagull V and another thank you to Carol de Solla Atkin for a last minute proof reading. We still have a good deal of further Supermarine seaplane information from the above contributors and others, an opportunity for further books. Any errors are our responsibility, and we are keen to receive readers' comments to help us to improve the content further.

James Kightly, Oxfordshire, September 2004.

Roger Wallsgrove, Hertfordshire, September 2004

Dedication

This book is dedicated to all the Stranraer and Walrus ground and air crews world-wide, who operated these machines in conditions ranging from the heat of the Sahara and the tropics to the sub-zero Arctic and Antarctic poles.

Development

Authors' note

This work is not intended to be a comprehensive history of these two aircraft – that book remains to be written. What is included is – we hope – enough information to put both aircraft into their historical and technical contexts. We also offer more technical photographs of both types than have ever been offered before in such a compact book.

Should the interest in this book be sufficient, we intend to produce a full history on the Supermarine Walrus, and (again if there is sufficient interest) another book on the Supermarine Stranraer. Both aircraft are unjustly neglected in the view of the authors. If you have further information, contributions or feedback we would be very pleased to hear from you. Please reply to the address in the front of this book.

The website www.shagbat.org is intended to act as a focus and forum for those interested in the Walrus and its crews. Any comments or suggestions triggered by this work can be directed to the website or to webmaster@shagbat.org as well as to the publishers.

List of Abbreviations:
ASR	Air Sea Rescue
FAA	Fleet Air Arm (of the Royal Navy)
D/F	Direction finder
MAEE	Marine Aircraft Experimental Establishment
MG	Machine Gun
RAAF	Royal Australian Air Force
RAF	Royal Air Force
RAN	Royal Australian Navy
RDF	Radio Direction Finding (later 'Radar')
RNAS	Royal Naval Air Station
RN	Royal Navy
Saro	Saunders Roe
TAG	Telegraphist Air Gunner
W/Op	Wireless Operator

Photo Credits:
Aeroplane	Aeroplane Magazine, London, England
APMA	Australian Plastic Modellers' Association
AWM	Australian War Memorial, Canberra, ACT, Australia
CanAv	Canada Aviation Museum, Rockliffe, Ottawa, Canada.
FAAM	Fleet Air Arm Museum, Yeovilton, Somerset, England
IKB Archive	Ian K Baker Archive, Australia
JDK	James Kightly
IWM	Imperial War Museum, Lambeth, London, England
RAAFM	Royal Australian Air Force Museum, Point Cook, Victoria, Australia
RAFM	Royal Air Force Museum, Hendon, Greater London, England
RMW	Roger Wallsgrove
Shearwater	Shearwater Aviation Museum, Dartmouth, Nova Scotia, Canada

Supermarine Walrus & Stranraer

Introduction

The Spitfire is, undoubtedly, the most famous aircraft produced by Supermarine and Reginald J. Mitchell. This rightful and unrivalled prominence has both overshadowed and distorted the nature and history of the work of both designer Reginald J. Mitchell and of the company which employed him. In light of this, it is perhaps appropriate to set the scene again.

From its inception, Supermarine was intended to be a company that produced marine aircraft, and from 1914 to 1939 that is where its primary work lay. Although the Spitfire and its progenitors, the S4, 5 and 6 in the later Schneider Trophy races, are well known and documented, these were exceptions to the long run of types that the company produced. Supermarine's core work was, in fact, producing versatile, basic, marine aircraft - either for private or early airline use on marine routes, or to provide the RAF with marine aircraft to extend and consolidate the Empire's reach.

R J Mitchell was highly regarded in the aero-industry as a seaplane designer, and his machines, almost without exception, were safe and successful – including our two subjects. They were among the world's best and were only occasionally let down by inadequate engines. They rarely reached too far, as the S4 did into the not yet understood realm of high speed flight.

Seagull V and Stranraer production line, Itchen works, 1939. Visible are two Stranraer hulls part-completed, and the two nearest Walruses are having their fabric, dope and markings applied in an area with copious 'no smoking' signs. (FAAM)

Introduction

Both the Walrus and Stranraer are examples of designs which were developed from a long string of previous aircraft. They were both designed at about the same time, although to fulfil very different tasks. Because they came from the drawing boards of Mitchell's team, it is not surprising that the resulting aircraft bear a number of similarities to each other, both in looks and equipment. The Walrus was the most successful of a long line of single-engine flying boats and amphibians produced by Supermarine and one could believe that if the helicopter had not been invented, the line might have continued until the present! The Stranraer, on the other hand, was the last of the big biplane maritime patrol boats produced by Supermarine, and World War II was the last operation for this type.

Due to the loss of much of Supermarine's early documentation (because of WWII bombing and a 1960's fire), there are still a number of gaps about many aspects of the company's development history. Coupled with the bizarre and often inexplicable nomenclature and type designation system of the Supermarine company, there are a few places where no sensible explanation can be offered as to what happened. And when we take a long view of an extended period of production – longer than an employee would have opportunity to do – we discover some naming overlaps fit to confuse the keenest modern enthusiast.

Pictures of British Walruses in the Far East are hard to find and many are anonymous. This aircraft is seen departing the deck of escort carrier HMS Khedive, in May 1945, with the late war two-blue roundel and white stripes in the wings and tail. (AWM A29251)

History

Development of Supermarine's single engined seaplanes

Walrus I W2706, of the RN/RAF combined Air Sea Rescue Flight, North Africa. This photo probably taken at Bu Grara in March/April 1943, when the unit was flying rescue patrols along the Tunisian coast during the Mareth Line battles. Note the pale wing float – possibly an aluminium-doped replacement, or perhaps painted white or yellow for enhanced visibility?
(IWM CNA 452)

Between 1919 and the flight of the prototype Seagull V in 1933, Supermarine produced a bewildering array of single-engined flying boats. Each of these was a development of the machine before, usually leading to the next design, but sometimes they were simply rebuilds using parts of the previous design, which were then renamed and sold again.

As we have seen, Supermarine were in the habit of developing successful (and not so successful) types into newer versions. The sequence of single-engine biplane flying boats is quite straightforward, although the variety of uses to which they were put is not so clear! Unclear too, is the rationale of the development of the Walrus from the Seagull V; a certain amount of surmise is necessary.

To consider the Seagull V we must look first at the Seagull III – which was itself actually only a variant of the Seagull II.

History

Walrus I (serial unknown) on board HMS Suffolk, June 1941. Note details of the hull shape, and the asymmetry of the nacelle mounting struts. (A4187(N) IWM)

Below:
Seagull V A2-9, believed to be flying off HMAS Australia, 1936. (Colin Owers via IKB archive)

History

The Supermarine Seagull V and Walrus.

In the inter-war period, the Australian armed forces were busy exploring, circumnavigating and mapping their otherwise uncharted continent, and principle among a range of types used for this was the Supermarine Seagull III. This was a wooden-hulled amphibian flying boat biplane with a tractor inline engine, the Napier Lion, and it provided an excellent platform for exploration and mapping even in the humid and challenging conditions of the Cape York peninsula and Great Barrier Reef. The Seagull III was a Seagull II that had been specially built for Australian requirements. Two marks differed only in minor aspects. In the late 1920s Supermarine devoted a certain amount of effort to producing a metal-hulled replacement prototype as a private venture, and called it the Seagull V. (The Seagull IV designation was used for yet another one-off design, which was never built.) It is possible that Supermarine was either led by the Australians (informally) to believe that there would be orders for this machine, when built, or they may just have been using spare design time - or they may have even had another, now-forgotten, use in mind.

In 1929, the Royal Australian Air Force drew up a specification for a machine to replace their Seagull IIIs. Unlike the machine in use, the new one should be "capable of catapulting with full military load" and of stowage and operation from HMAS Albatross, a seaplane tender and a base for a half dozen Seagull IIIs – not an aircraft carrier as we now understand it, and Australia's

Seagull III in RAAF Service – though very different looking to the Seagull V and Walrus, it is clear here that the overall configuration is essentially the same. (Photo courtesy of Rod McWade via APMA)

History

Seagull V serial number A2-7, of No. 9 (Fleet Cooperation) Squadron RAAF embarked on an unspecified modified Leander class cruiser of the RAN being positioned on the catapult: the aircraft's original role. Note the extended leading edge slats (unique to the Seagull V) on the upper wing, the lack of jury struts inboard between the wings, the spoked uncovered wheels, and what is probably a thermometer or barometer attached to the port forward engine strut. (IWM 044443)

first home-assembled warship. The requirements and specification were demanding. When they were sent around the wide selection of British aircraft firms, Supermarine was just one of the companies to receive the specification. As we have seen, Supermarine had just the thing under development. In 1933 it had been pushed to the back of the workshop due to more pressing demands, but the RAAF Chief of Air Staff, Sir Richard Williams, managed to persuade Supermarine to get going again and on 21st June, 1933, after a burst of activity to finish the prototype, the Vickers Supermarine Seagull V launched from Southampton Water for the first time, in the hands of chief test pilot 'Mutt' Summers.

At this stage the Australians were committed to the type; they had a role for it (exploration) and were clearly prepared to buy a batch. The British, in the form of the Director of Technical Development, went on record as stating; "Very interesting; but of course we have no requirement for anything like this." (One of those highly regrettable phrases that in fact is not as stupid as hindsight indicates.) However, this lack of official British interest was to be overturned by two factors. First, the RAAF arranged for the Marine Aircraft Experimental Establishment (MAEE) at Felixstowe, Suffolk, to evaluate the prototype – and when the British tested the machine for the Australians, the result was that information on the type came into official British circles. Secondly, in the early thirties there was quite an arms race on in terms of capital ships - a key component of which was that they should have some form of airborne reconnaissance machine.

The tests were very successful, and the Australians got the 24 Seagull V machines they wanted. The Royal Navy decided that there was something in it after all, after borrowing some of the Australian machines to try out, and they ordered a batch (to be named Walrus rather than Seagull V – for no good or clear reason we know of) for use aboard Royal Navy cruisers and

History

Flight of Walruses over Malta before W.W.II. Note that the lead aircraft's upper wing is heavily patched, that they all bear the wing walk "footprint" markings, and that aircraft '069' has the spotting hatch open above the cockpit.
(FAAM)

battleships. These were ostensibly to spot the fall of shot, not unlike the first use of warplanes on land in 1914, but they were used in many other roles, including fishing trips for the Admiral and surveying previously unexplored parts of the world (and the Empire).

The Walrus was to see a brief period of success in its envisaged role as a spotter for the fleet, in the early war period of 1939 and 1940. In particular, Walruses helped to hunt German commerce raiders in the wide seas, both in Royal Australian Naval service (the Seagulls being Royal Australian Air Force operated) and Fleet Air Arm Walruses operated for the Royal Navy.

The campaign in Norway demonstrated how much the British forces had to learn (or re-learn) in warfare, but the Walrus was a weapon which demonstrated a remarkable adaptability in extreme circumstances. Undoubtedly one of the last times a Commander in Chief has taken part in a battle was when Admiral Lord Cork, during an airborne assessment of the war zone,

A very wet Seagull! Though apparently about to sink, this was normal working conditions for Seagulls and Walruses. Early style aluminium dope finish, with "footprint" wing walks.
(Colin Owers via IKB archive)

History

L2228 *"Spotter of Spartivento", about to be launched from HMS Sheffield. May 1941. Note the name is only carried on the starboard side of the nose, despite what has been published elsewhere.*

(IWM A4049)

was able to throw a bomb overboard onto a rail line – perhaps not changing the course of events, but providing some satisfaction in a particularly frustrating campaign.

At the Battle of Spartivento, a Walrus played its expected role in a fleet-to-fleet engagement, but radar (RDF at this stage and still a secret) had in many ways taken this job away from aircraft. Warships were also discovering that they needed all the anti-aircraft weaponry they could gather on their upper works. Some use of spotter aircraft was very effective in extending the scope of the Admiral's battle intelligence, but the situation in which the reports of the spotting Walrus were relayed back to the battleship via Alexandria don't show the Navy working at its most efficient!

The Walrus' initial fleet-to-fleet engagements in the Mediterranean theatre fitted the expected pattern of the 'fleet spotter', but after the Royal Navy came under increasing pressure from land-based forces and the Luftwaffe, the Walrus' job became both redundant and highly risky. In maritime skies unexpectedly filled with single-seat enemy fighters, whether in the Mediterranean, Pacific or Indian Ocean, the Walrus' days were clearly numbered. By 1943, all fleet cruisers in the Royal Navy and Royal Australian Navy had their catapults removed and extra anti-aircraft guns fitted, radar having replaced the Walrus itself.

The eclipse of the role of 'fleet spotter' coincided with a new need for an Air Sea Rescue facility, as we shall see below; but that was far from every-

History

Unique shot of Walrus of HMS Norfolk under tow to Murmansk, as referred to in the text. (FAAM)

thing that the Walrus was good for. Any amphibian would find itself useful in wartime – the Walrus was that, and had further assets in that it was very seaworthy, could carry a significant load or a number of passengers, and was reasonably armed for both defensive and offensive roles. Like many wartime aircraft that did not get to spend significant time in the limelight, many Walrus exploits went almost unrecorded. Those exploits that we are aware of are all the more amazing as they have been overshadowed by other events. The Walrus, a bizarre looking machine, and a biplane that seemed out of place in a predominantly monoplane war, was often caricatured by the press of the day, which detracted from the deadly serious work it undertook.

Walruses were used in secret operations, as well as acting as dive bombers, fighters (in an extreme pinch!) as well as the apparently mundane roles of reconnaissance and communications (as originally expected) – they even helped distribute the Navy's mail. The scattering of Convoy PQ17 (from Britain to Russia) in July 1942 left HMS Norfolk's Walrus (out on patrol and unable to receive messages) powerless to find any of the ships on its return to the rendezvous point. After a no-doubt panicky search, they finally located one of the merchantmen and, landing alongside, received a long tow and lift to Murmansk.

That the Walrus was specified to undertake dive bombing is not too surprising, as the Lords of the Admiralty seem to have been keen it could do everything, with the possible exception of launching a torpedo or flying in fighter combat. What is remarkable is that it did actually act as a dive bomber, in the Madagascar campaign (also strafing two fortresses) used by a crew and commander whose feat in remembering that it was supposedly part of the Walrus' job description was as amazing (no doubt) as the actual attack!

Despite its obsolescence in the role of 'fleet spotter', the usefulness of the Walrus had been demonstrated in many ways. When the battle between Britain and Germany, in 1940, unexpectedly occurred over water, clearly something was needed to recover airmen from the sea. It appears that, although the pre-war RAF had a number of small water craft for marine aircraft use, and experienced airmen supporting marine aircraft, the assumption was that the Navy would look after downed flying crew. The reality was quite different in the desperate days of 1940. The first rushed answer of the air sea rescue (ASR) launches were a start, but they couldn't get to a downed airman as quickly as an aircraft. Arriving overhead with a dinghy pack in a Boulton Paul Defiant or Westland Lysander (unwanted by Fighter Command and Army Co-Operation, respectively) was only part of the answer – being able to alight and actually pick up the swimming man was clearly the next step, and a vital one if hypothermia was not to claim another life. So a handful of Walruses were borrowed from the Navy, and although they were initially intended only for rescues in mild seas, the men of the ASR flights began to set a superlative standard of bravery, airmanship and seamanship which has become famous as the Walrus' finest hour, although it is not often realised that this service only really got going after the Battle of Britain was over. What is also not well known is that this rescue work quickly spread to the Mediterranean and Far East, where the Walrus was the machine of choice again.

Some rescues occurred in minefields, or under the guns of the enemy just off the coast of France. Often the Walrus became overloaded when picking up a complete bomber crew, and would have to taxi back to port or hand over the rescued airmen to another vessel and make another attempt to get airborne. Each and every rescue was important, and many of them were dramatic and unique. However, we will take just one famous rescue to illustrate this role. Wing Commander Duncan Smith ended up in the sea after his fuel-tank switch failed him after a reconnaissance just before the invasion of Italy. Baling out on the morning of September 2nd 1943 at 2,000 feet, he lost his boots in the drop and was only lightly clad in short-sleeved shirt and shorts. He also got a cut leg on the way down - his dinghy having been lost, he was in the water supported only by his 'Mae West' - a precarious position. Despite swimming for shore, he was in a current and after a couple of hours, he was beginning to get the apparently bizarre combination of both hypothermia and sunburn. Though his position had been pinpointed by another Spitfire pilot when he bailed out, the searching Spitfires were unable to find him where expected, until a Rhodesian named Shand acted on a hunch and over-flew Smith, over 5 hours after he had gone in. Interestingly, Shand had himself been rescued by a Walrus in April.

Famous shot of a flight of ASR Walruses of 751 Squadron, Dundee airborne over Scotland during 1943. Surviving Walrus W2781, although not in this picture, did serve with this unit.
(FAAM)

History

Interior of a Supermarine Walrus amphibian aircraft of No. 277 (Air Sea Rescue) Squadron RAF in 1945. The two beds and electrically heated jacket are used to thaw rescued airmen.
(AWM UK2402)

The first Walrus that had set out had developed engine trouble and returned to base, but the second, flown by Sergeant R Brown with Flying Officer Dick Eccles and Flight Sergeant Jack Berry aboard as crew was on its way. After the usual difficult open water landing, a rope was thrown to Smith, and he was hauled aboard – to be smacked in the back of the neck and knocked out by a bullet from an attacking enemy fighter. A melee had developed over Smith and the Walrus, and several Messerschmitt Bf109s, Focke-Wulf Fw190s, Macchis and a Regianne 2001 were tangling with the escorting Spitfires. One Spitfire was shot down and the pilot killed, and a 109 claimed in return, while the Walrus was badly holed and Brown was trying to get out of it post-haste. While Berry held his hands over two major bullet holes in the hull spurting water, and Eccles held his arms over his head ("to ward off the cannon shells!" as he recalled) Brown hauled the aircraft off – despite another cannon shell through one fuel tank spurting petrol over the engine and exhaust. As ever, amazingly, after being dragged off the sea at 40mph, the Walrus made it back to base Milazzo, where it was condemned as scrap. Wing Commander Smith was patched up and soon returned to service.

The Walrus soldiered through the War in the ASR role, also performing tasks where nothing else would do. Several Walruses found quirky new roles in civilian hands after the war, as well as new military opportunities. Walruses were used as whale spotters, light feeder-liners and pleasure craft, and while they were not successful in any of these roles for the long term, their use did mean that some Walruses survived.

History

Left:
Admiralty Islands, Pacific Ocean. September 1944. Pilot Don Watson (far right) was based with 71 Wing for air-sea rescue duties. This aircraft carries a mermaid on its nose art, apparently with the name 'Rescue Girl'. Note the replacement front to the nacelle, possibly still in primer.
(AWM P00279_027)

Below:
Aircraft and crew of 284 Sqn RAF, the first ASR unit operating from Sicily in 1943. Third from left in the front row is WO Norman Pickles, awarded the DFC for bravery under fire after he was hit during a pick-up at sea. Note the variation in 'uniform' permitted in this theatre.
(IWM CNA.1186)

History

Walrus survivors

Supermarine Seagull V A2-4 is, as its serial would indicate, the oldest surviving member of the Walrus family. After military service it passed into civilian hands, serving as a seven-seat 'airliner' among other roles, but was damaged in 1970 in a take-off in Taree, NSW, Australia. Traded for a Spitfire XVI it passed into the hands of the RAF Museum in 1973, where it was rebuilt and refurbished. Despite a long and active life, and damage to the port aft fuselage requiring repair, by RAF Wyton and the RAF Museum restoration centre, Cardington, it was remarkably complete. Refitted with military equipment from the RAF Museum's collection, it was put on display in 1979 in the Battle of Britain hall at the RAF Museum Hendon. It has been there ever since, in its early war camouflage.

Seagull V VH-ALB in its Amphibious Airways Charter scheme in Queensland post-war and (below) now in the RAF Museum Hendon.
(JDK collection & Mark Ansell.)

History

*Top: the Fleet Air Arm Museum's Walrus L2301 in its civil scheme on a south coast beach (FAAM) and **below**, as it is displayed today.*

(Mark Ansell.)

The Fleet Air Arm Museum's Walrus Mk.I L2301 also had a fascinating career, serving throughout WWII with the Irish Air Corps as N18. Amongst other excitement, its working life included being the subject of a failed hijacking attempt. Following a brief postwar career as G-AIZG, it (sadly) ended up in open storage at a scrapyard in Thame in 1947. After loss of a significant number of parts, it was finally obtained by the Fleet Air Arm Museum in 1964 from the Historical Aviation Preservation Society who had rescued it. RNAS Arbroath rebuilt it (a major task requiring a significant number of new parts) and delivered it to Yeovilton in December 1966, where it has remained on public display ever since.

Walrus Mk.I W2718 was discovered in the disguise of a 'home-made caravan'! It was obtained by Dick Melton, who had been scouring the world for an example to restore to airworthy condition. Despite a resemblance to the Walrus fuselage, the caravan yielded only a starting position for an extensive ground-up rebuild. All of the major parts have been obtained or fabricated by Dick and his team over a number of years. At the time of writing the fuselage is a complete unit, though without fittings and systems.

History

Top:
Another view of L2301, this time with wings spread.

Bottom:
Dick Melton's Walrus project (G-RNLI/W2718) seen on display at Popham in the early 1990s.
　　　(Both Mark Ansell)

The (complete) project, registered G-RNLI on Carol Melton's (Dick's wife) suggestion, is up for sale and awaiting a buyer to complete the task of putting the only Supermarine marine aircraft back into the air.

While the last Australian Seagull resides in the RAF Museum in Britain, the last Walrus survivor - HD874 - is proudly displayed in the RAAF Museum, Point Cook, in Australia. Chosen to form an aerial reconnaissance component of the 1947 Australian National Arctic Research Expedition, it managed one photographic flight before being rolled into a ball by 90mph winds just before Christmas at Heard Island, Antarctica. Abandoned there, it was brought back in 1980. A ten-year restoration was completed in early 2002, putting this rare machine back into its Antarctic overall yellow scheme. Built by Saro, it is often incorrectly identified as a Mk.II. However, it is a metal hulled Mk.I, the Mk.II type being extinct.

History

Top:
The Australian Arctic Survey's Walrus lies wrecked after its one and only flight at Heard Island, where it was abandoned. (RAAFM)

Middle:
In the restoration hanger at Point Cook (JDK) and bottom, as rolled out after an eight-year restoration at RAAF Point Cook.
(RAAFM)

History
Progeny

The wooden-hulled Mk.II Walrus was designed by the sub-contractors Saunders Roe, who had taken on Walrus production because Supermarine were fully occupied with Spitfire production. One of the little ironies was that the Southampton I was a wooden-hulled machine, and in order to save weight, the Mark II had a metal copy of the wooden hull form – exactly the reverse of the Walrus!

As is ever the case, ideas that would define the successor to the Walrus were already being explored at the time the Seagull V and Walrus were entering Australian and Royal Naval service. This was the Sea Otter, looking very much like a tidied-up Walrus with the engine, a Bristol Mercury, now a tractor (i.e. 'pulling': often regarded as the 'right' way around). Due to the urgency of Spitfire production and the shift of Walrus production to Saunders Roe from Supermarine, the Sea Otter's development and production was severely delayed.

The Walrus had proven, like several other simple adaptable machines, to be a stalwart. Despite a few attempts to update or replace it, it was cheap and available enough to make replacement attempts relatively futile. The Sea Otter had never overtaken the Walrus in service because it did not offer a significant enough performance improvement (just as the Fairey Albacore failed to replace the Swordfish).

At the war's end, the final shot came from Supermarine's marine locker. The Seagull ASR Mk.I was built to a 1940 specification, S.12/40, first flying on 14 July 1948. This was a totally new type, but without any mark number to differentiate it from those Seagulls that had gone before. It was intended for the ASR role, and the original specification included carrier hanger restrictions, though these were later dropped. It looked like the result of a night of passion between a late Griffon-engine Spitfire and the Walrus, featuring a huge amount of mechanical complexity in a variable-incidence wing with

The Supermarine Sea Otter is often mistaken for a Walrus, however as long as the engine (tractor, not pusher) is visible, no mistake should be made. Here RD872 is about to land on an HM Carrier, after the war.
(Aviation Photo News)

a multi-part flap arrangement – more adaptable than today's airliners. Had the helicopter not matured as quickly as it did after the war, the Seagull ASR might have found a role as a 'plane guard' picking up aircrew whose aircraft went over the side of their carrier. A sleek-looking machine, it had a phenomenal speed range: a highly creditable top speed of 241.9 mph won it the World's Air Speed Record for amphibians over 100km while, at the other end of the speed regime test pilot Mike Lithgow could loiter the machine at a mere 35mph – quite slow enough for most purposes! However, the helicopter could do a better job in the ASR role and the Seagull ASR was single-engined, and had a negligible sized cabin and payload compared to the Grumman amphibians that were the competition in the light amphibian market in this period. Two prototypes and a half-finished third machine were all that emerged.

Top:
Civil registered Sea Otter G-AKRG gradually returning to nature.
(Aviation Photo News)

Below:
The post-war Supermarine Seagull ASR at Farnborough. Last of the line, this sleek machine saw its role taken over by the helicopter despite an enormous speed range and remarkable performance.
(JDK collection)

Walrus Mark identification.

The Walrus was used in a wide variety of roles and in as extreme a range of climates as the earth can provide, yet the layout did not change from the first prototype to the last machine built. There were only two hull types: metal for the Seagull V / Walrus Mk.I, wooden for the Walrus Mk.II. Otherwise the only differences lie in which fittings were bolted on or taken off. Despite this simplicity, Walruses are often misidentified, but close study of the photographs and plans presented here will clarify this differentiation. Sadly, all of the plans the authors have seen so far are incorrect in many aspects, and excepting information from the aircraft's own handbooks, most published information is to be treated with suspicion. To clarify, we therefore present a list of the differences.

Seagull V prototype.

Essentially a hand-built one-off, the first of the line has a number of features which are unique to it and it alone - helpful when one considers the number of schemes it went through, as well as the number of photographs taken of it!

Fuselage: a pointed top to the bow, rather like a liner's prow. All subsequent Seagulls and the Walrus Mk.I had a rounded bow, with the two mooring bollards at a distinct angle. A teardrop faring to the undercarriage junction (properly 'chassis' in this period). No fold-up screen above the 2nd

Top:
Seagull V prototype marked as N-2 (originally marked as "N-1"). Subsequently allotted the RAF serial K4797.
(RAF Museum P13374)

Right:
Lt Commander Caspar John in the cockpit of the Seagull V prototype being hoisted aboard HMS Courageous in Portsmouth Harbour at the start of the first sea trials in February 1934. Numerous details are worth identifying, including the two compasses mounted on the bow, and the non-standard (for later Walrus and Seagull V) ladder for access to the engine.
(FAAM)

History

Top: Previously believed sunk after its non-fatal crash in Gibraltar Harbour in January 1936, this formerly unpublished photograph proves that the first Seagull was recovered, but as can be seen here the damage resulted in the aircraft being written off. At this stage it had been brought up to Mk.I Walrus standard, but still retained the 'N' tail struts, different shaped fuselage window, and fairing for the undercarriage leg. (A.E. Mitchell, via Jo Mitchell.) Lower: This magnificent photo of the prototype, in happier days in the Mediterranean, shows a good deal of detail, including the open canopy windows to allow for some cooling breezes through the aircraft. (FAAM)

pilot's position. Almost square observer's window either side, rather than the elongated rectangle of the production machines. 'N' strut arrangement supporting the horizontal tailplane. No 'jury' struts on the inboard forward part of the interplanes when the wings spread. No Handley Page slots on upper wing leading edge. Potts air cooler on upper starboard section of the engine nacelle.

Other items: Pictures show the prototype with an inter-plane ladder fitted forward of the upper centre section, rather like that fitted to larger flying boats

History

(Stranraer etc.) instead of the footsteps which folded out from the struts, as on all subsequent machines. As built, there were no catapult spools by the step or on the rear fuselage (fitted later). A Scarff ring is evident in some early shots, rather than the dedicated Supermarine mounting. There appears to be a 'ladder mat' fitted to the lower wing stubs in some pictures presumably to assist in moving around on the aircraft when on the water. A larger square water rudder (soon replaced with the kidney shaped unit) was the first tailwheel/water rudder arrangement. There is a picture showing hand compasses fitted simultaneously either side of the front gunner's position, and the distinctive thermometer cover familiar on the port nose area of the Walrus was not fitted.

Seagull V

Twenty-four were built, for the Australians. A number of minor equipment differences existed, but because the Australians received replacement Walruses as the Seagulls were written off, the equipment fit soon became uniform. However, the Seagull was originally fitted with Handley Page slots on the upper wing, and the interplane jury strut was intended to be removed when the wings were spread (but it was not vital that they were removed, so it did fly with them fitted!) All Seagulls (except the prototype) were given and retained 'A2-xx' serials. Australian Walruses normally retained their longer British five digit alphanumeric serial, which helps with this difficult area of identification.

Supermarine Seagull V being approached by a boat to take off the crew in pre-war Australian service. Note the port upper wing has been heavily patched and the roundel has not yet been fully repainted. This picture also shows the 'at rest' waterline position clearly.

(AWM)

Walrus Mk.I

Derived from the above type, there were no Handley Page slots on the upper wing, the bow was rounded, with angled bollards, and the observer's window was an extended rectangle shape, sometimes later fitted with a windscreen. There was a sub-window inset to the 2nd pilot's upper forward windscreen, to be raised as a windscreen when taking compass bearings for fall-of-shot spotting. The original tailwheel was an all-metal affair encased in a flat kidney-shaped water rudder. A tarmac landing (rare in the 1930s) apparently sounded like 'the collapse of the Forth Bridge'. Not surprisingly, many Walruses were retrofitted with a Sea Otter type pneumatic tailwheel, usually without a water rudder casing. The wing jury-struts were permanently fixed on the Walrus Mk.I and Mk.II.

Left:
W3085 "B" about to catapult off HMS Mauritius, 1942. The wing-walk markings are clearly visible, as are the ASV radar aerials.
(IWM A9272)

Below:
The First Seagull V for the RAAF taxiing at the RAF Hendon Display in 1935, bearing its 'new aircraft number' 11 on the nose. Absent are the inboard jury struts visible on the Walrus Mk.I in the picture above.
(JDK collection)

History

The variety of Walrus schemes: **Upper:** *A Fleet Air Arm Walrus with the upper wing roundels freshly painted out and a US Star over the fuselage roundel, as used during operation 'Torch'. (FAAM).* **Middle:** *Part of a sequence of press photographs, of a North African ASR unit, this shows well-worn Walrus K5782, with part of its water rudder missing, in what is believed to be desert camouflage, and with a light coloured float – possibly yellow or white. (AWM MED0042).* **Another picture of Walrus L2228**, *"Spotter of Spartivento" about to be hoisted aboard HMS Sheffield. The precarious nature of the TAG's job in climbing up to the top centre section even in mild calm weather is clear here. (IWM A4053)*

History

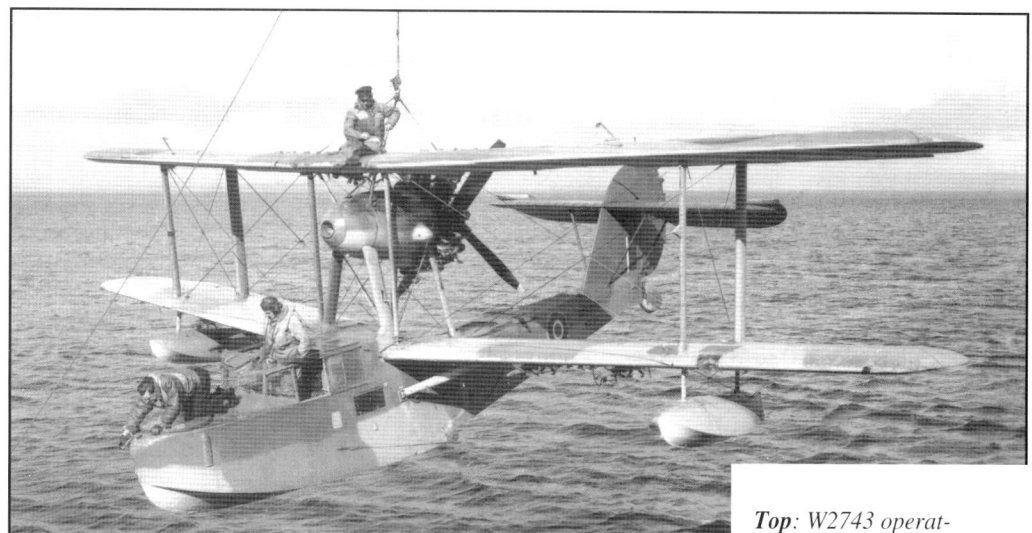

Top: W2743 operating off HMS Pegasus, a catapult training ship. Lamlash, Scotland, Sept. 1942. Notice that the four colour camouflage on the hull, often easy to miss, is clearly visible here. (IWM A 12035) **Middle**: Walrus YQ-H of No.9 (Fleet Co-op) Sqn, late 1943/early 1944. Believed to be Extra Dark Sea Grey/Dark Slate Grey with Sky Blue codes and undersurfaces, and RAAF roundels. (Colin Owers via IKB archive) **Bottom**: Walrus I of 712 Sqn coded G9G being pushed back for takeoff after landing aboard a carrier; although not equipped with a hook, Walruses were able to land aboard with little difficulty. Ship and aircraft unknown. Note the upper camouflage extends over all of the engine nacelle. (RAFM P2310)

History

Walrus Mk.II

Fitted with the Saro-built wooden hull. Although Saunders Roe built all the Mk.II Walruses, not all Saunders Roe Walruses are Mk.IIs - and many pictures claiming to be of Mk.IIs are in fact Saro-made Mk.Is with the metal hull! The wooden hull is quite easy to identify - there is a hard chine line at the upper quarter of the rear fuselage, rather than the rounded panel edge on the metal machines. The line from the cockpit windscreen to the bow (common to all machines) slopes downwards on the Mk.II rather than being horizontal as on the metal hull. The resulting panel arrangement and front gunner's position are very different on the Mk.II and the bow is pointed rather than rounded - although different from the Seagull V prototype. The wooden hull did not, of course have rivets (despite some recent drawings claiming that it did!) and the arrangement of panel lines is different - if almost invisible in most photos. There were prominent inspection portholes on the rear fuselage / tail of the Mk.II. Most Mk.IIs were used for air sea rescue and training, and the ASR machines sprouted grab rails etc. However this was not unique to the Mk.II, many Mk.Is also being so fitted when in the same role. Likewise, the fitting of airborne radar was a function of role rather than mark.

Photos which really do show Mk.II Walruses are hard to find. Top: Walrus BA-D of 277 Sqn, Digby, 1944 (RAFM P5016) Below: Pegged out to graze. Walrus Mk.II HD925 awaits being "reduced to produce" with a couple of Sea Otters behind anticipating the same fate. Again, details of the different construction of the Mk.II wooden hull are easy to see on close examination, as is the faded but still distinct four colour camouflage, used even at this late stage.
(RAFM P1625)

Technical details:

Supermarine Seagull V

Engine	1 x 625hp Bristol Pegasus IIM2
Span	46'0"
Length	38'0"
Height	15'0" (on undercarriage)
Wing Area (Sq ft)	610
Empty weight (lbs)	4,640
Normal all up (lbs)	6,847
Max speed (mph)	125
Cruise (mph)	95
Initial climb (ft/min)	900
Endurance	600 miles at 95 mph 3,500 ft.
Range (miles)	634
Ceiling (ft)	15,500
Armament	2 x .303in Lewis MG, 1,000 lb bomb load
Production:	24 supplied to Australia, 1935 – 1937, A2-1 to A2-24

Supermarine Walrus I (II)

Engine	1 x 625hp Bristol Pegasus IIM2 (1 x 750 hp Bristol Pegasus VI)
Span	46'0" (45'10")
Length	38'0" (54'10")
Height	15'2" (15'3") (tail down, on undercarriage)
Wing Area (Sq ft)	610
Width folded	17'6"
Undercarriage track	7'7"
Propeller dia	10'0"
Empty weight (lbs)	4,640 (4,900)
Normal all up (lbs)	6,847 (7,200)
Max speed (mph)	125 (135)
Cruise (mph)	(95)
Initial climb (ft/min)	900 (1,050)
Endurance	600 miles at 95 mph 3,500 ft.
Range (miles)	634 (600)
Ceiling (ft)	15,500 (18,500)
Armament	2 x .303in Vickers K MG, 760 lb bomb or depth charge load

Production

Total 285 all Supermarine built Mk.I metal hull. K4797, prototype Seagull V (Previously N-2 and then N-1) K5772 – K5783; K8338 – K8345; K8537 - K8564; L2169 – L2336; N9 – N-14 to Turkey; N-15 & N-16 to Argentina; P5646 – P5670; P5696 – P5720; R6543 – R6557 –X1045 wooden hull Mk.II prototype; X1046 believed not built.

History

Saunders Roe production - 271 Mk.I: R6582 – R6591; W2670 – W2689; W2700 – W2729; W2731 – W2760; W2766 – W2798; W3005 – W3051; W3062 – W3101; X9460 – X9484; X9498 – X9532; X9554 – X9558. 190 Mk.II. (From above Mk.I batches the following believed built with Mk.II wooden hull: W3010; W3047; W3051; W3076; W3078) Mk.II production: X9559 – X9593; Z1755 – Z1784; Z1804 – Z1823. HD804 – HD837; HD851 – HD878; HD899 – HD936. total: 1 Seagull V, 555 Walrus Mk.I, 191 Walrus Mk.II.

Construction

The Supermarine Walrus Mk.I was a single-engine biplane tractor amphibian of mixed construction. The fuselage was all metal stressed skin configuration, with an integral lower fin. It was built on a fuselage profile jig: the frames were inserted and then stringers and panels were added. The undercarriage had hydraulic retraction arms set into the fuselage sides. The main wheels retracted into wood-lined recesses in the lower wings. Positions for a single pilot (with optional dual controls), wireless operator, navigator and observer were fitted out. There was a forward gun position which could also be used for mooring, as well as a central gun position, which was often used for access. The tailwheel was normally enclosed in a water rudder. The engine, a Bristol Pegasus, was positioned midway between the fuselage and the upper centre section. It had an integral oil cooler and tank in the engine nacelle; the thrust line being two degrees offset to starboard. The wings were metal spars with metal ribs interspaced with wooden ribs, fabric-covered with areas of ply reinforcement. The small upper fin and the whole of the horizontal stabilizer and elevator were wooden construction with stainless steel fittings. The rudder was metal with fabric covering. Fuel tanks were fitted in the inner ends of the upper wings.

The Walrus Mk.II differed only in having a wooden fuselage, made in the same shape and configuration as the metal unit (with the detail differences described earlier). The wooden fuselage required a slightly different nose contour, tail fuselage junction, and bonding strips for electrical connections.

History

Supermarine's multi-engine flying boats

As we have seen with Supermarine's single-engine flying boats, there was a clear development thread running through a confusing naming system. As one might expect, the same applies to the big multi-engine flying boats of R.J. Mitchell.

While there were a number of successful machines before it, the Supermarine Southampton was a revolutionary and extraordinarily successful machine. The Royal Naval Air Service knew that large flying boats could be effective due to the successes of the Felixstowe types in WWI, but a period of inadequate design and use was ended by the one-off Supermarine Swan. Confidence in the concept was regained and the Air Ministry even ordered the Supermarine Southampton design off the drawing board, -and into production, without going through a prototype stage. Their confidence was well rewarded by one of aviation history's best designs. First flown in 1925, the Southampton was a conventional layout twin-engine wooden-hulled flying boat. The incorporated refinements in design were from a long string of earlier types, and although design refinements such as tank-testing still lay in the future, Mitchell and his team had come up with an aircraft which (according to its crews and to the RAF) was an ideal compromise. With the efforts of the crews, the RAF was able to expand the possibilities of the long range maritime patrol boat, cruising the Mediterranean, Baltic, Far East and even as far as Australia – no simple feat with the relatively-limited facilities of the 1920s! In company with offerings from the other manufacturers of Britain's marine aero-industry, a 'golden age' of big biplane flying boats developed in the 1930s. The pace of change was rapid. The development from Southampton I to Stranraer occurred within a 10 year period. This

RAAF Supermarine Southampton I wooden hull with the tail of a Seagull V in the foreground at RAAF Point Cook in the thirties.

(IKB)

History

development culminated in the superlative Stranraer before design focus switched to monoplane machines.

The wooden-hull Southampton was replaced with a metal-hull version, the Mk.II of 1926. It was then able to avoid the weight penalty of water-soak that all wooden flying boats were prone to – a saving of 500lb in construction weight and 400lb in water soak, meaning that the Mk.II could carry more or go further. Perhaps more surprisingly, the opportunity appears to have been missed to take the metal monocoque design principles back to the landplanes of the period, which might have resulted in arriving at the principles that were later pioneered by companies in the United States.

In this period, even the best designs did not receive a great production order, so Supermarine reworked the Southampton concept for a number of potential clients. Southamptons ended up in some unlikely hands, geographically spread as far as Argentina, Australia and Japan. A three-engine derivative was built for the Norwegians, called the Nanok, as well as a civilian version, the Solent. (Not to be confused with the later Short Solent.) Almost all of the boats to date had been configured around the wooden monocoque design based on a system known as the Linton Hope type. This comprised an essentially cylindrical cigar shape to which the shaped planing bottom and the chines for spray suppression were added on externally.

The success of the Southampton led Supermarine (now supported by Vickers Armstrong's hydrodynamic facilities after Supermarine's takeover by the combine in 1928) to explore another development, originally named the Southampton IV. This was a clear step away from the wooden Linton Hope design (the Southampton Mk.II was effectively a metal 'remake' of the wooden hull's shape) and a number of explorations and corrections in design resulted in a new hull configuration. After a very successful tour of the prototype (still named Southampton Mk.IV) through the Mediterranean in 1933, the Air Ministry ordered twelve of these machines, to be renamed Scapa.

Stranraer prototype K3973 chops through the waves on takeoff.
(Aeroplane)

History

The Stranraer

The pace of development in this period can be very well illustrated by the fact that Mitchell designed an altogether bigger type based on the Scapa work, but with a 12% increase in wingspan, area and weight. Powered by the moderately supercharged Pegasus IIIM, the performance was such that it was able to exceed the performance of any other British flying boat in its class. Even more telling of the rapid development and better structured and more analytic approach to testing was the fact that the Stranraer's larger hull managed to match the hydrodynamic performance of the Scapa's in tank tests at St Albans.

With war clouds gathering, the Air Ministry ordered seventeen Stranraers. Their eyes were on the newer machines that were due for wartime use, such as the Sunderland and Lerwick. The Stranraer was a very workmanlike aircraft in RAF use, coming as we have seen after a long line of flying boat reconnaissance machines. A flight of five Stranraers of 228 Squadron took a 4,000 mile cruise in 1938, culminating in exercises with the Mediterranean fleet from Malta, after staging through Lisbon and Gibraltar - very much in the model of the Southampton's earlier cruises. However, while the RAF were getting maximum benefit from their 17 machines with service in four squadrons and two training units, the crews would have been looking to the much more modern monoplane aircraft which were in service during the Stranraer's era. Remarkably quickly, these more modern machines had

Interminable hours were spent by Stranraer crews on patrol. Stranraer 922 is prepared for a particularly long one, as the long-range overload tank can just be seen below the port wing. This aircraft was burned and sank at its mooring at Alliford Bay, B.C. on New Year's Eve, 1941, due to 'carelessness'.

(Shearwater)

Supermarine Walrus & Stranraer

History

Pre-war Royal Canadian Air Force Stranraer on the step.
(Shearwater)

eclipsed the biplane boat and its era to the degree that the Stranraer Squadrons began regarding themselves as second class citizens. Despite important work in 1939 and 1940 patrolling the sea between Norway and Scotland, based at Invergordon, the Stranraer was replaced as quickly as possible. The last operational flights were in the spring of 1941. The last RAF survivor (K7303) was noted for the final time in October 1942.

The Stranraer might just have been a footnote in Supermarine's history, were it not for the desire by the Dominions to start manufacturing aircraft to equip their hastily-expanding forces. The assumption was that licence-built designs were all that the colonials would be able to manage at this stage. Canada was expected to look to Britain rather than to the United States of America for its designs, and Vickers in Montreal was set up to build the Stranraer as a licence-built design. By the end of the production run, having overcome a number of major obstacles including shortages of engines, the St Laurence river freezing mid-production, and tackling a highly demanding production challenge previously unknown in Canada, the Canadians had produced forty Stranraers. They were issued to Canadian units on both coasts of North America, and remarkably, a number of them flew across the huge continent as a change of deployment. When they were eventually phased out it was in favour of the Canso, a Vickers Canada built Consolidated Catalina, alongside which they had served when the first Cansos were introduced.

Reaching the pinnacle of biplane flying boat excellence was, of course, a mixed blessing. Performance requirements resulted in the development of monoplane types and their subsequent monopoly. Long-range cruisers such as the Consolidated Catalina took advantage of the high aspect-ratio wing to gain the advantage previously held by the biplane. While the top edge performance of the Stranraer could be beaten by the newer flying boats, its carrying ability, robustness and seaworthiness gained great loyalty from its Canadian

History

The similarity to the Supermarine Walrus can be seen clearly in this shot of a Stranraer under construction in Montreal. The keel-jig method was also the same as used in Walrus construction. Good detail of the cross section of the hull and the chine flare can be discerned.

(CanAv)

crews in particular, a number of whom regarded their Stranraers as better in this arena than the popular and successful Catalina and Canso line.

While the maritime patrol work of the Royal Canadian Air Force Stranraers never hit the headlines in the way that the fighter and bomber squadrons did, the seemingly-endless hours of monotonous patrol, inconclusive sightings, and hardship were vitally important to ensuring Canada's coasts and shipping weren't attacked. Although U boats and surface raiders proved elusive, the weather and sea were always there and were usually unsettled, at best. The environment therefore showed little mercy, and the requirement to patrol whenever possible put these brave crews regularly in situations in which the Stranraer's slow speed, robust biplane layout, and remarkably reliable engines were all critical survival aids – though sometimes even this was not enough.

If the Stranraer had not been chosen for licence production in Canada, it would probably have remained a little-known interim type and although, the Canadians did end up licence-producing the much more effective Catalina afterwards, the Stranraer found a popular and useful niche in patrolling the Canadian seaboard, and later opening up the West coast islands to air transport (in civilian hands).

No less than fourteen of the Canadian Stranraers joined the Canadian civil register – the most famous operator being Queen Charlotte Airways on the west coast of British Columbia, provided a tramp-steamer style service to the isolated camps in this rugged island chain. The last survivor in this demanding service was CF-BXO, which after ceasing service in 1958 and passing through a number of users, has ended up in the RAF Museum, Hendon as the sole survivor of its type and a lone complete representative of the pre-war multi-engine flying boat.

Supermarine Walrus & Stranraer **37**

History

Technical details:

The Supermarine Stranraer

Engine	2 x 920hp Bristol Pegasus X (Canadian production 2 x Bristol Pegasus XXII, some later converted to Pegasus X and Wright Cyclones. Prototype: 2x 820hp Bristol Pegasus IIM)
Span	85'0"
Length	54'10"
Height	19'9" (21'9" on beaching gear)
Wing Area (Sq ft)	1,457
Empty weight (lbs)	11,250
Normal all up (lbs)	19,000
Max speed (mph)	165
Cruise (mph)	105
Alighting speed	58.5mph
Initial climb (ft/min)	1,350
Endurance	9hr 3min
Range (miles)	1,000
Ceiling (ft)	18,500
Armament	3 x .303in Lewis MG, 1,000 bomb or depth charge load

Production

1 prototype, K3973 delivered 1934. 17 delivered K7287 – K7303 delivered between 1937 and 1939. 40 built Canadian Vickers. S Nos 907-916, 918-923, 927-938 and 946-957 delivered between 1938 – 1941

Construction

The Supermarine Stranraer was a twin engine metal biplane flying boat of conventional layout. The fuselage was of stressed-skin metal construction throughout, with bulkheads at regular intervals with access doors at a height to enable some planning-bottom damage control. The forward fuselage was heavily flared into integral chines for spray suppression. The cockpit had positions for two pilots, a flight engineer and a navigator stations, while there were gun positions in the nose, mid-fuselage and tail, as well as a bomb aimer's position in the nose. A good deal of extra equipment was carried to enable the aircraft to work while away from its main base – including a curtain to separate the "officer's quarters" from the "airmen's"! The two engines (Bristol Pegasus X) were slung underneath the upper wing, at the end of the centre section, faired by long chord Townend cowlings. Initially, two-bladed wooden propellers were replaced by four-blade wooden units, and finally by Fairey-Reed metal three-blade configuration. The lower wing stubs were built integral to the fuselage, and the deck area above them was clear for externally-carried equipment for ferrying purposes. All flying surfaces were fabric covering over Alclad parts with stainless steel fittings. Anodic treatment was also undertaken to assist in the process of corrosion resistance. The single horizontal elevator was configured with offset aerodynamic balances. A three-point beaching gear was provided, with a trolley for the rear of the planning-bottom and a strut-braced single wheel unit for each side. Canadian and British beaching gear appears to have been of different construction, but attached to the same points on the aircraft.

Below: An 'Honour Guard' of Stranraers was provided for the departure of King George VI and Queen Elizabeth from their Canadian tour in 1939. Keeping marine aircraft clean around the waterline, even on such a prestigious job, is difficult! Those who know Halifax, Nova Scotia will be able to pick out many familiar details including the Halifax Citadel, now a major tourist attraction, just in front of the aircraft's nose. 909 survived the war to be lost on a mercy flight near Port Simpson, B.C. when operated by Queen Charlotte Airlines as CF-BYL "Skeena Queen". (Shearwater) **Lower**: Although a poor quality photo, this shows RAF Stranraer K7287 running up engines presumably after test, and reveals a good deal of the clutter surrounding such activities, including the engine servicing platforms rigged below the uncowled port engine. (Aeroplane)

History

Select Bibliography:

The Stranraer Aeroplane (Boat Seaplane) Two Pegasus X Engines 1st Edition, 1937 AIR 10/2091, The National Archives (Formerly the Public Record Office)

The Walrus I Aeroplane (Amphibian) Pegasus II.M.2 Engine 1st Edition 1936. AIR 10/2079, The National Archives (Formerly the Public Record Office)

The Walrus I & II Aeroplane (Amphibian) Pegasus II.M.2 Engine or Pegasus VI Engine 2nd Edition 1943 (Reprint) AIR 10/2081, The National Archives (Formerly the Public Record Office)

Andrews, C.F. & Morgan, E.B. 1981. Supermarine Aircraft Since 1914, Putnam. 0-370-10018-2

Bassett, Ronald. 1988. HMS Sheffield – The life and times of 'Old Shiny'. Naval Institute Press. 0870214349

FAA Museum. Jan 1967. Shagbat. Control Column Magazine.

Franks, Norman. 1994. Another Kind of Courage. Stories of the UK-based Walrus Air-Sea Rescue Squadrons. Patrick Stephens Limited. 1-85260-441-7

Franks, Norman. 2003. Beyond Courage - Air Sea Rescue by Walrus Squadrons in the Adriatic, Mediterranean and Tyrrhenian Seas 1942-1945. Grub Street. 1-904010-30-X

Hall, Alan W. April 1986. Aircraft in Detail - The Supermarine Walrus. Scale Aircraft Modelling Magazine. Vol.8 No.7.

London, Peter. 2003. British Flying Boats. Sutton Publishing. 0-7509-2695-3

Morgan, Eric et al. April 2001 Database, The Supermarine Stranraer. Aeroplane Monthly Magazine.9770143724132

Nicholl, G.W.R. 1966. The Supermarine Walrus. Foulis.

Scale Models Staff. July 1979. Supermarine Stranraer. Scale Models Magazine. MAP

Weight, Chris. 1997. Jericho Beach and the West Coast Flying Boat Stations. MCW Enterprises. 0968115802

Wilson, David. 1991. Alfresco Flight – The RAAF Antarctic Experience. Heritage Series, RAAF Museum. 0-642-10522-7

Detail photos

WALRUS
Fuselage

Above:
Late war far eastern markings can be seen as well as many other details, as a RAAF detachment on board HMAS Australia at sea in February 1943 ships the landing wheels on the Walrus prior to its being catapulted.
(AWM 029510)

Left:
Sole surviving Seagull V A2-4 at the RAF Museum, Hendon.
(RMW)

Detail photos

Clockwise from top: The bow of RAAF Museum Walrus HD874 peeks from the restoration hanger (JDK) while the crew of a Walrus respond to the press photographer's wishes (IWM A4186). The hull of Dick Melton's Walrus G-RNLI gives a good idea of the overall shape and the picture of HD874 shows the flat panel but still complex shape of the forward planning hull.

(Both JDK)

Opposite page:
Port & Starboard views of HD874. The starboard lower wing and tailplane have been covered in a clear film to show the details of the aircraft's mixed construction as well as the fuel tank, which is left in bare metal in the upper wing.

(JDK)

Detail photos

Detail photos
WALRUS Exterior

Opposite page:
The rigging diagram from the Walrus manual.

Top:
The TAG mounts an ammo pan on the Lewis gun. The mounting is the patent Supermarine pillar track device. The heavily riveted nature of the fuselage is clearly evident.
(IWM A4183)

Middle:
The planning hull of G-RNLI seen from port-aft looking forward.

Bottom:
The roundel and mooring rope on A2-4.
(Both JDK)

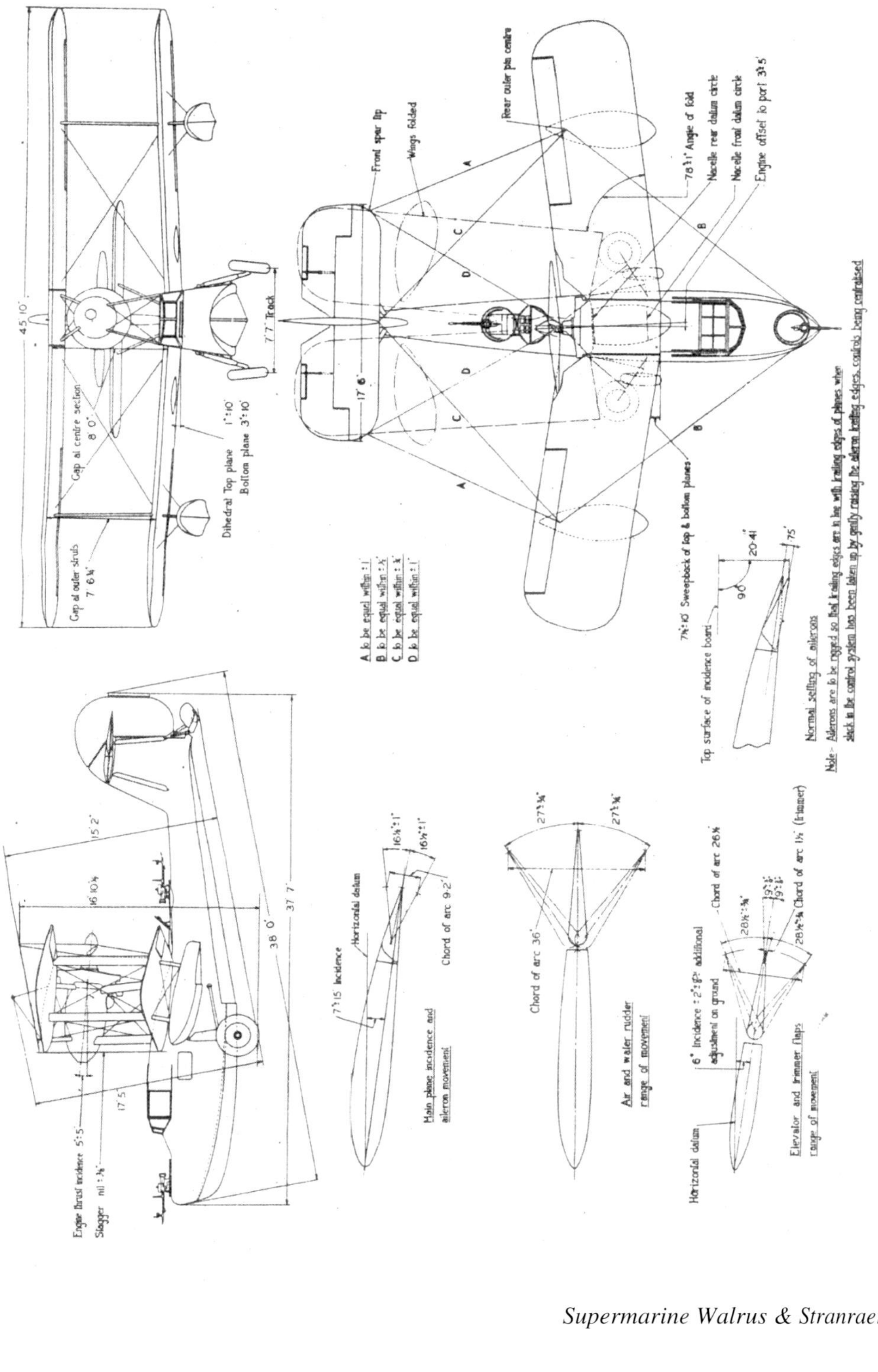

Detail photos

FIG. 143. GENERAL ARRANGEMENT & RIGGING DIAGRAM

Detail photos

Clockwise from top: The rear fuselage of G-RNLI shows its cross section. (Keith Saunders) At Jacquinot Bay, New Britain, April 1945 this Walrus used by 10 (Comm) Flt, RAAF, has its wing fabric repaired by airmen, showing the wing's construction. Left to right: Corporal Riddell, L/A L.H. Roberts and Corporal N. Bliss. The stencil style of squadron codes is clearly visible as are the ASV aerials on the upper centre section. (AWM OG2441) The noses of A2-4 and (bottom left) L2301 show details of the bollards and the undercut of the outer section of the planning hull. (Both JDK)

Detail photos

Clockwise from top left: The nose of A2-4 appears to have a side panel that is unique to this machine. (JDK /RMW) The instruction panel for wing folding, fixed to both sides of the fuselage. (JDK) The lower wing-fuselage join, rigging and strut detail. The mooring bollards and nose hatch surround, all on A2-4 (JDK / RMW) Chartboard in hand, the navigator prepares to board an FAA Walrus 'somewhere at sea' aboard a carrier. (IWM)

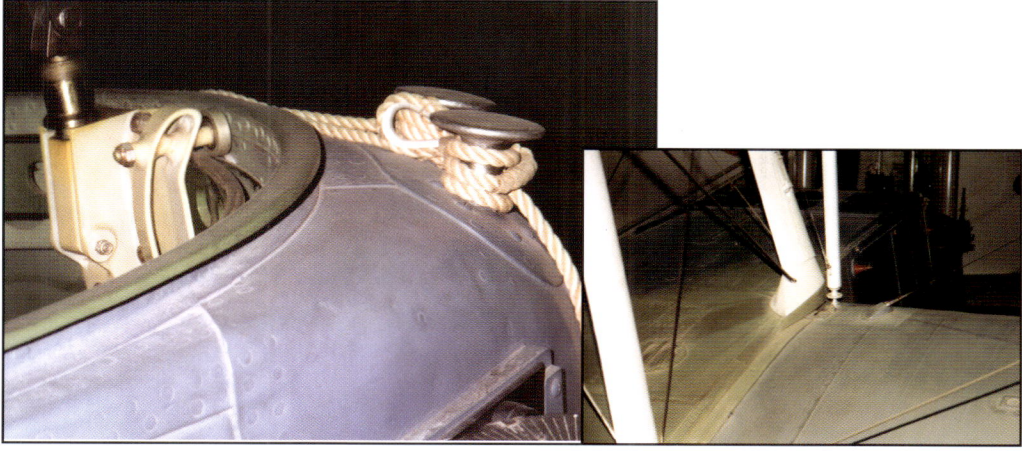

Supermarine Walrus & Stranraer

Detail photos

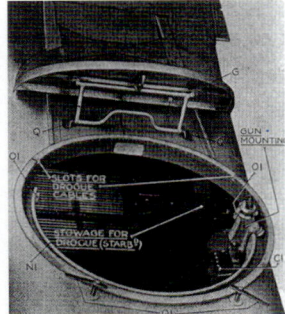

Details of the aft hatch cover from the manual and on A2-4. (RMW)

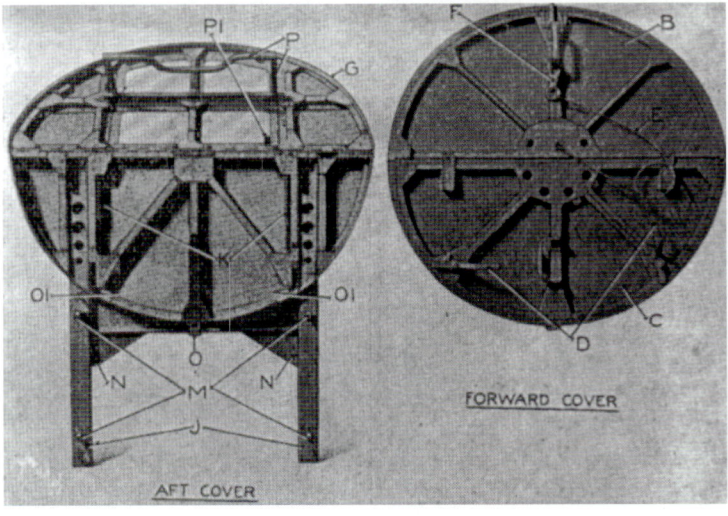

48 *Supermarine Walrus & Stranraer*

Detail photos

From top right: *The aft catapult spool on the rear fuselage of L2301. The D/F loop fitted specially to HD874 for its Antarctic survey work. The external compass mounting, and end of the mooring line. (all JDK) The nose art on a Walrus attached to No.10 Squadron RAAF at Mount Batten, 1940. (Abstate Subter is bad Latin for 'Look out Below'!) Details of this aircraft are elusive, as the Squadron was a Sunderland unit, it is conjectured that this might be a Squadron 'hack', and Walrus L2312 was issued to this unit, though it is not certain it is this machine. (AWM 044944) Two pictures of the characteristic thermometer housing and mooring rope.*

(JDK)

Supermarine Walrus & Stranraer **49**

Detail photos

Lower part of the fuselage of W2743 operating off HMS Pegasus, a catapult training ship. Lamlash, Scotland, Sept. 1942. (IWM)

The nose of HD874, with its metal hull. The distinctive shape of this area is quite different on the Mk.II wooden aircraft. Below right: The nose hatch cover. Bottom right: The fuselage roof below the engine. The engine inspection porthole and its protective bars are visible in the centre.

(All JDK)

50   *Supermarine Walrus & Stranraer*

Detail photos

The rear hatch in situ (top) and being slid forward and raised (middle). Bottom left: The small tiedown latches recessed just forward of the tail. Bottom right: The step, radius arm of the undercarriage, and forward catapult spool on the port side of HD874. The catapult spool fitting is over-painted here as the aircraft was not used in the catapult role, but was often left as bare metal, being a stainless steel fitting.

(All JDK)

Supermarine Walrus & Stranraer

Detail photos
WALRUS Wings

Above: The port lower wing from the manual, showing the large number of fittings required.
Below: The starboard tank of HD874, with the gravity feed visible at the bottom right. The tank would normally be covered, although it is exposed here for display purposes. (JDK)

Detail photos

Details of the lower wing fold joint and latch on L2301. Note the often-overlooked folding flap which rotates upwards to allow the wing to be swung back. It was not a landing flap, as is often conjectured, and on the prototype Seagull V, it actually folded down.
(All JDK)

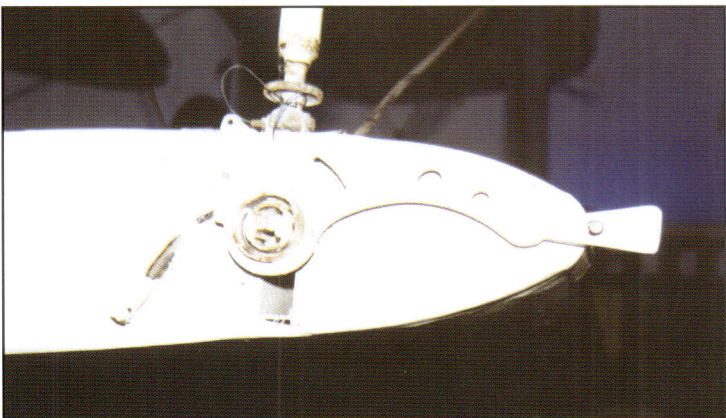

Below:
A Seagull V about to be launched from a RAN cruiser, showing details of the catapult and trolley, and the position of the underwing 'A' of the serial.
(Colin Owers via IKB archive)

Detail photos

  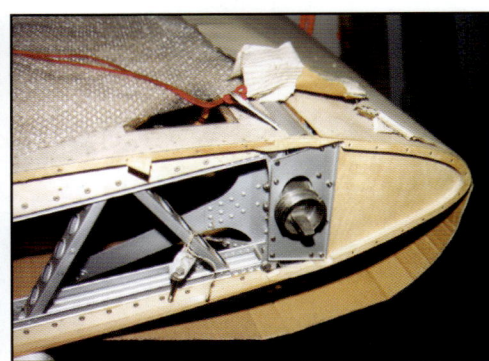

Clockwise from top left: The pitot head on L2301. Open cover on flap latching mechanism, starboard lower mainplane, A2-4. Detail of the upper centre section of G-RNLI, still in cardboard. The interior of the wheel-well on A2-4, with the cable operated uplock latch visible. The wing spars intended for G-RNLI showing the wing-section and cut-out for the stores racks. Early style landing light on A2-4.
(All JDK / RMW)

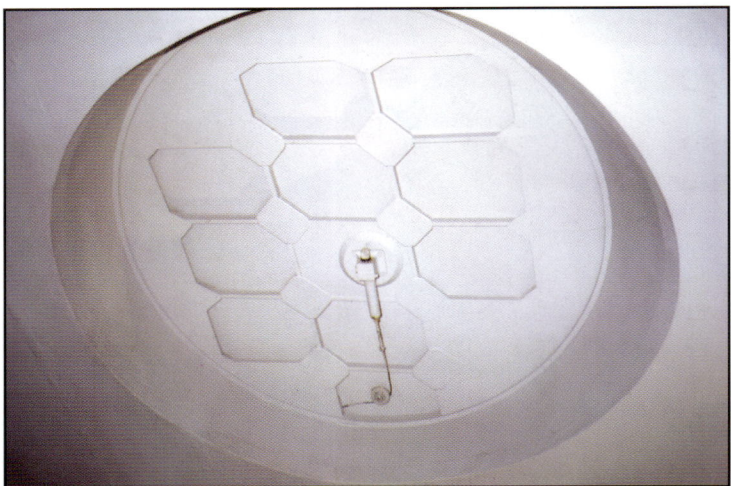

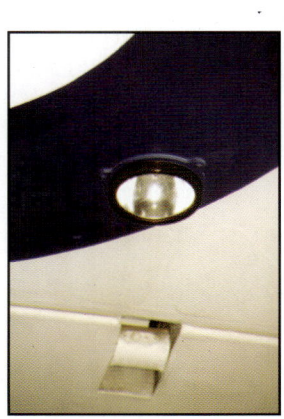 

Detail photos

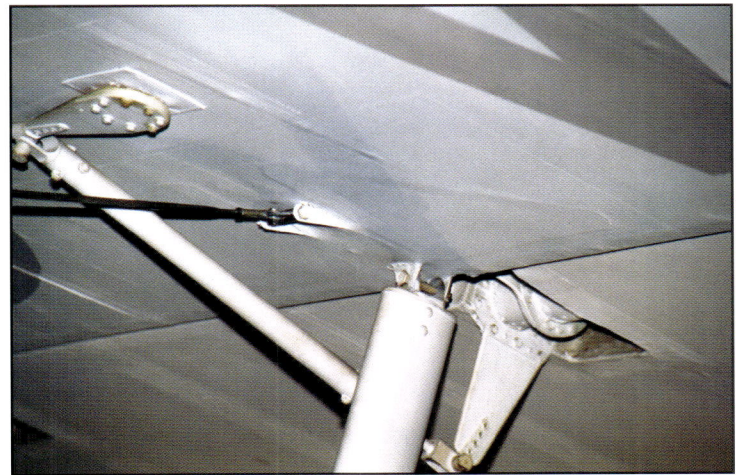

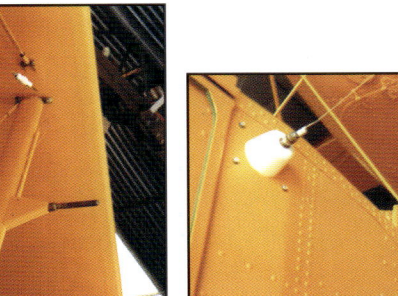

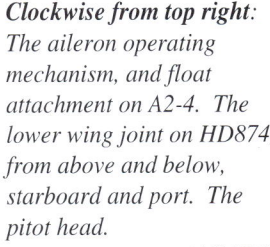

Clockwise from top right:
The aileron operating mechanism, and float attachment on A2-4. The lower wing joint on HD874, from above and below, starboard and port. The pitot head.

(All JDK)

Left:
Bombed-up with smoke floats, this SEAC marked Walrus gathers speed to get off the deck of HMS Ameer, after transporting a Hellcat pilot back to the carrier on 8th July, 1945. The pilot had been rescued 200 yards off the Japanese coast according to the original caption. Note that the pilot's quarterlight is open and the cockpit cover is slid back.

(FAAM).

Supermarine Walrus & Stranraer

Detail photos

The leading edge light on HD874; details of the port upper and lower wing-fuselage joints. Note the port fuel tank is covered, although the fairings over the centre section struts are not fitted. (All JDK)

Detail photos
Tail WALRUS

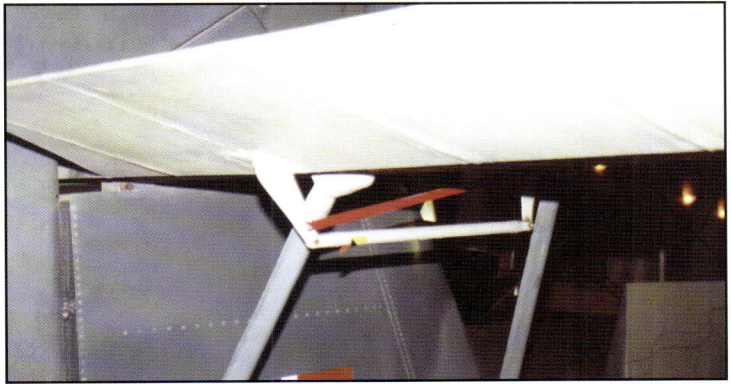

Details of the tail of L2301, and A2-4 (bottom). Note that the horizontal tailplane is a single piece unit, while the upper part of the fin is fabric-covered, and the lower section is integral with the hull.
(All JDK)

Detail photos

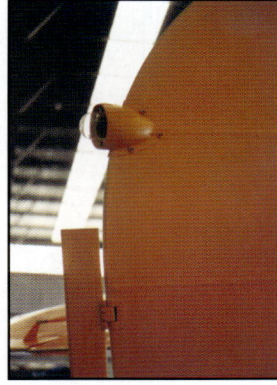

More details of the tail: A2-4 and HD874. The taillight and trimtab are visible (top left) and A2-4's small tiedown latch is lifted up at the right of the photo.
(All JDK)

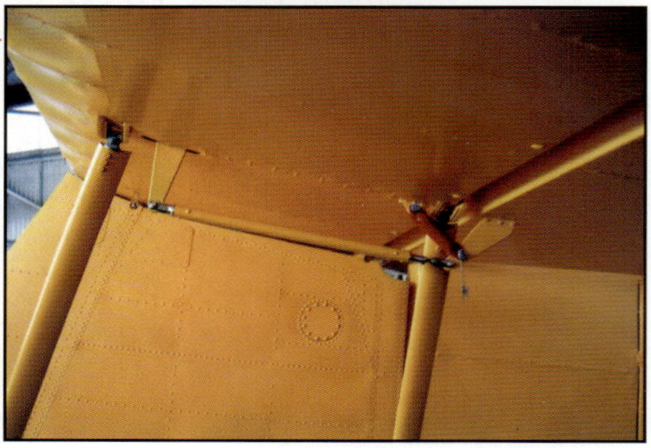

Detail photos

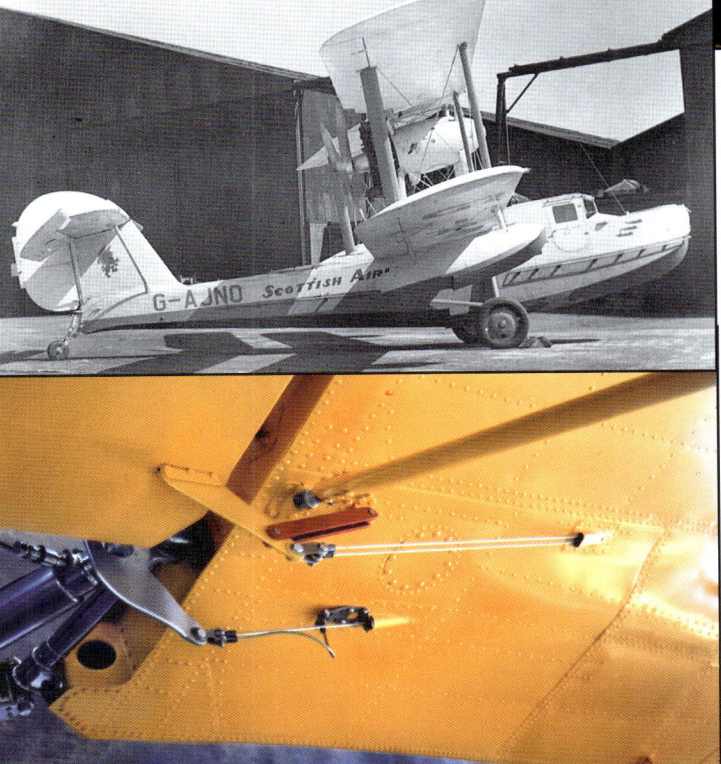

Tail details of HD874. Walrus G-AJNO of Scottish Airlines in civilian hands. Despite the extensively converted cockpit, with a new entry door, and snazzy scheme (believed to be white and orange) it was apparently never put to use. (JDK collection.)

Supermarine Walrus & Stranraer

Detail photos
WALRUS
Stores

The rear hatch of A2-4. The red bar is to stop unauthorised access, and was not an original fitting! A set of practice bombs (sometimes smoke bombs) fitted to the smaller rack of A2-4. (All JDK / RMW)

Below: *The ineffective early war anti-submarine bombs being loaded onto a Walrus, in 1939 or 1940. A large number of details can be seen, including the undercarriage bay and bomb racks, as well as the clothing and equipment of the RN crew. Note also the large fin flash and unusually-placed code letter (F) on it. (JDK collection)*

Detail photos

The patent Supermarine gun-mounting, here on A2-4. The course-setting bombsight fitted to A2-4 – rarely if ever used in practice. The deflection-compensating gunsight fitted to the aft machine-gun of A2-4.

(All JDK/RMW)

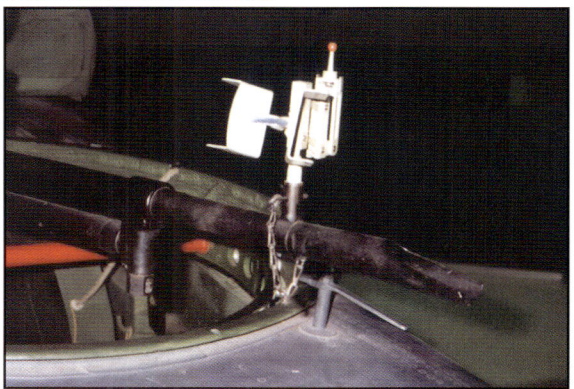

Supermarine Walrus & Stranraer

Detail photos

Top to bottom:
The Vickers K on the nose mounting of A2-4. Another view of the course-setting bombsight fitted to A2-4.
(Both JDK/RMW)

Walrus (X9564?) "Z" being hoisted aboard HMS King George V during Arctic operations, February 1943. Note ASV radar aerial on the upper wing leading edge and interplane struts, also that the main undercarriage has been removed: this was commonly done to save weight and increase patrol endurance.
(IWM A15441)

Detail photos
WALRUS Cockpit

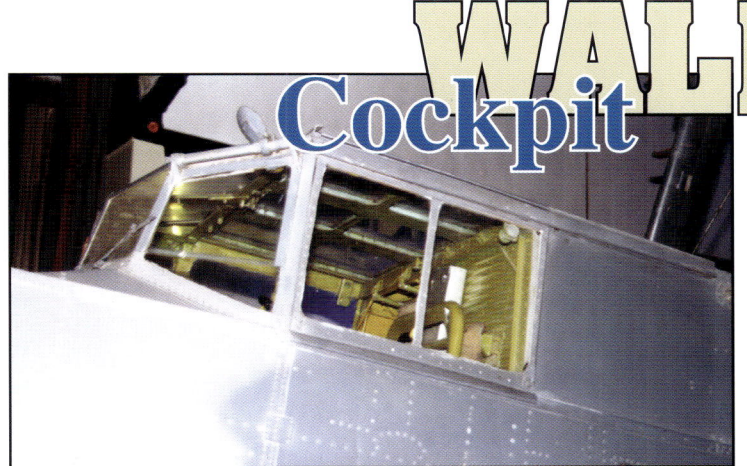

Two views of the cockpit of A2-4. There were minor variations, but the design stayed essentially the same. (Both JDK/RMW)

A photo of one of the Argentinean Navy Walruses, supplied post-war. A good view of the catapult trolley and mountings, and a small penguin badge on the nose. (FAAM)

Detail photos

The cockpit of HD874 as it was on Heard Island. Interior and exterior of the glazing of A2-4. (RAAFM) Note that the whole of the cockpit roof slides aft, seen here half open. The lack of the inset upper opening hatch (see opposite) in these pictures shows that this is a later replacement canopy. The rear-view mirror and windscreen wipers are of interest.
(Both JDK/RMW)

64 *Supermarine Walrus & Stranraer*

Detail photos

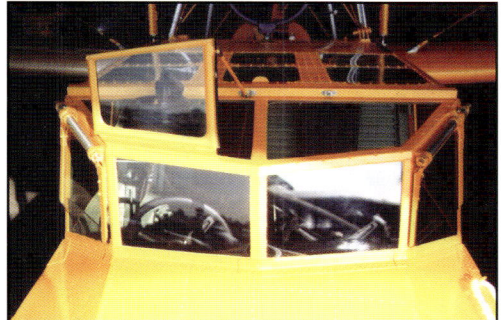

Multiple views of HD874's glazing, with the fall of shot compass fitted inside the erected 'windscreen'. Note the substantial hinges on the quarterlights. The control column on L2301.

(All JDK)

Supermarine Walrus & Stranraer 65

Detail photos

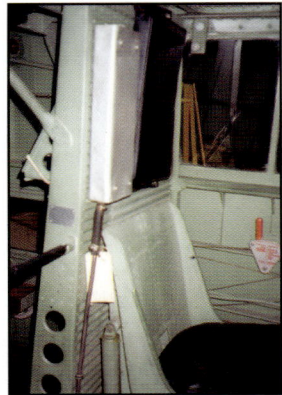

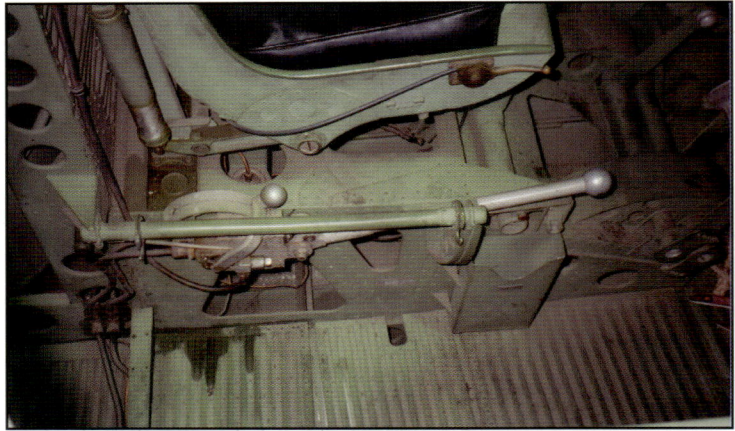

Pilot's position in A2-4. Bottom: The bare cockpit of G-RNLI showing the construction.
(All JDK/RMW)

Detail photos

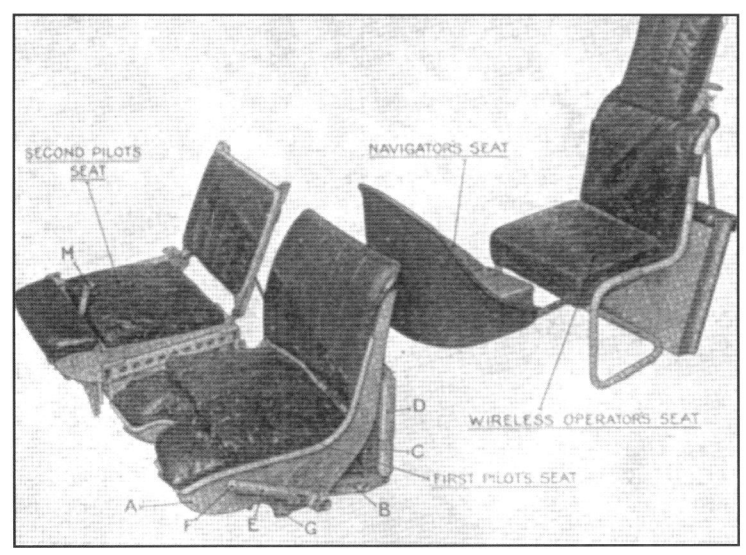

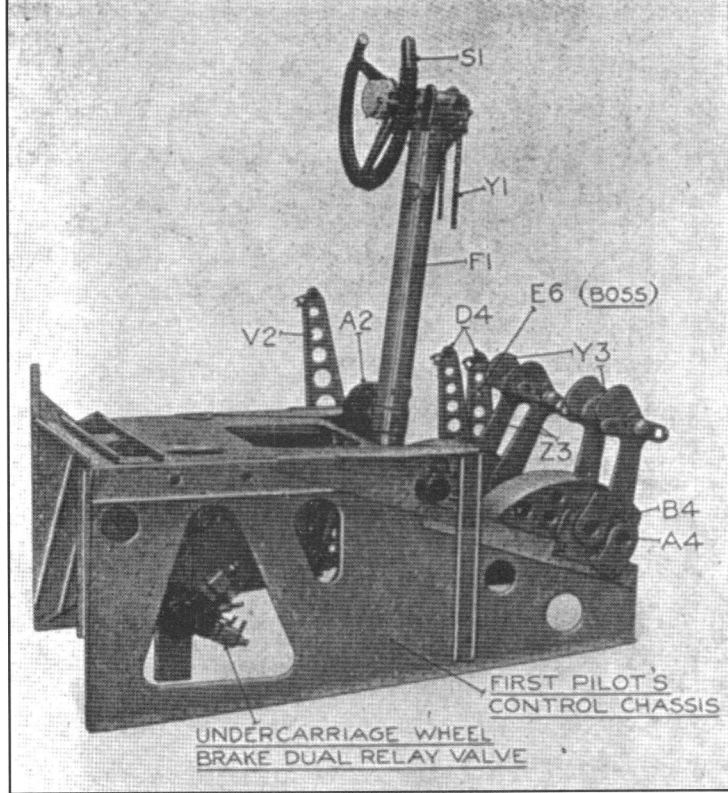

From the manual; Upper: the crew seats as arranged in the aircraft. The co-pilot's seat was able to be dismantled and folded away as it was in the gangway. Lower: The unit which carried the pilot's seat, control column, and rudder pedals.

Detail photos

Opposite page:
Top: Walrus P5658 was photographed here with an impressive array of rescues all presented in little lifebelts on the nose. One save of seven people was a Fortress crew.
(FAAM)

The instrument panel of HD874 from front and rear. Although complete, the instruments lack wiring and connections, so the rear is much tidier than it would be in an active aircraft!
(Both JDK)

Top: The trim and throttle controls of A2-4, (RMW) and lower: the early style instrument panel (without the standard six instrument blind flying insert) from the manual.

68   Supermarine Walrus & Stranraer

Detail photos

Supermarine Walrus & Stranraer

Detail photos

Contrasting panels of Walruses. **Top**: *L2301 (JDK),* **Middle** *A2-4 (RMW), and* **Bottom**: *a service machine. (IWM A19539)*
Many minor variations between the three aircraft are visible, some due to their original production date, others due to modification in use and restoration. Note, however, that the lower machine does have the Victorian bellpush fitted on the left!

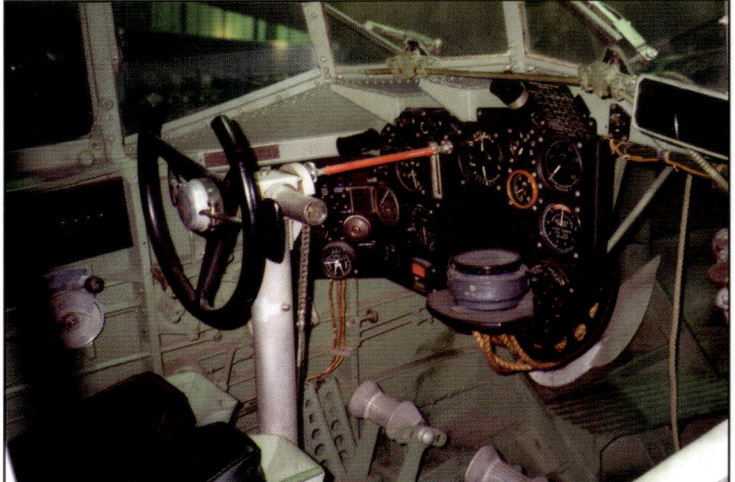

70 Supermarine Walrus & Stranraer

Detail photos
WALRUS Interior

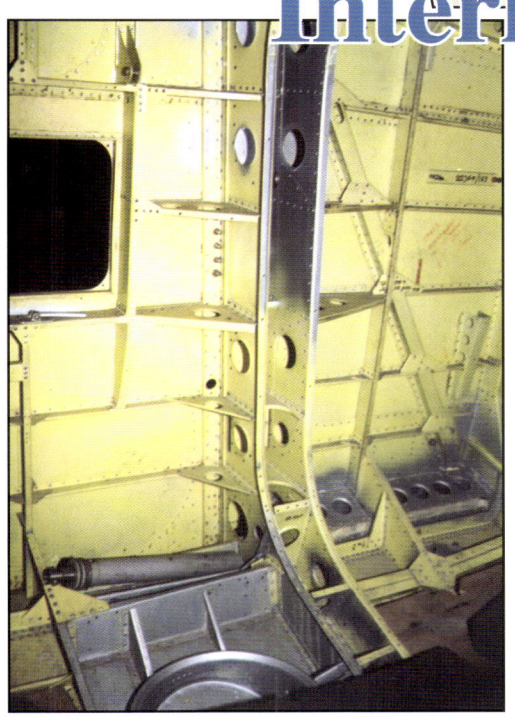

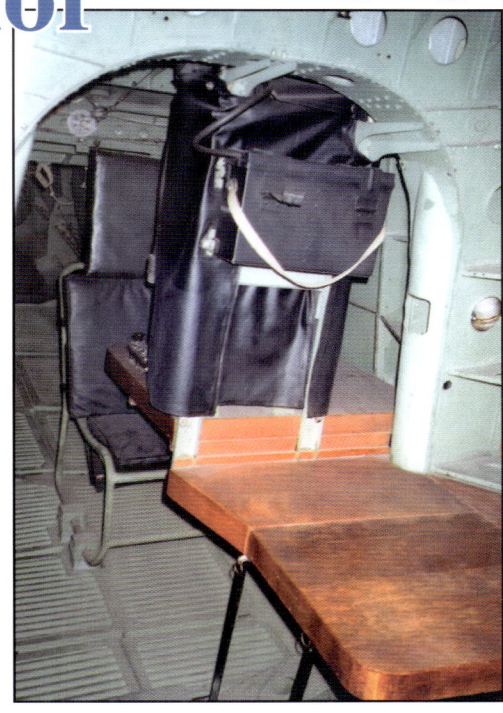

Top left: The hull interior, of G-RNLI, bereft of fittings but showing the double frames around the undercarriage retraction jack position. (JDK)
Top right: The chart-table and W/Op position in HD874, looking aft from the co-pilot's seat. (JDK)
Lower right: A navigator at his desk aboard a carrier-based FAA Walrus, looking forward. The co-pilot's seat is in the stowed position, and the wooden bilge walkways are fitted. (IWM A4180).
Bottom left: The bow compartment of G-RNLI, showing clearly the frame sections.

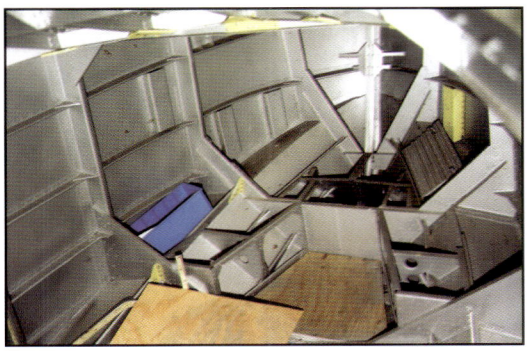

Supermarine Walrus & Stranraer

Detail photos

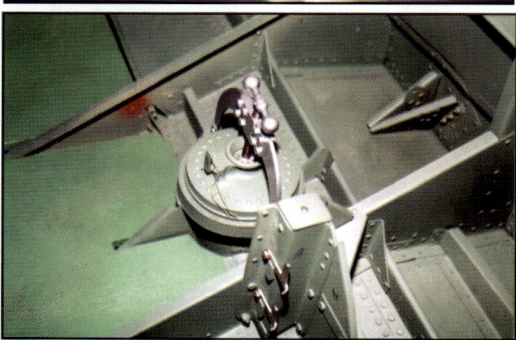

This lovely clear photograph shows a host of details of an operational Walrus, probably, going by the number on the radio, W2676. Below the radio-back is the Aldis lamp and compass. On the left hangs a binocular case, and behind the W/Op (working the Morse key for the press photographer!) the crew's parachutes and the interior of the rear fuselage can be seen. The other photographs in this series are on pages 42, 44 & 71. (IWM A4181) Details in HD874 from this area: bottom right: the trailing aerial wheel; bottom left, the small hatch in the hull floor; and left, the signal pistol port. (All JDK)

72 Supermarine Walrus & Stranraer

Detail photos

Clockwise from top: The rear fuselage interior of HD874, with the circular drogue case on the right, and the control runs behind that. The nose bollards, and extreme nose interior; the camera mount (when not in use) and the hatch for the camera port. (All JDK)

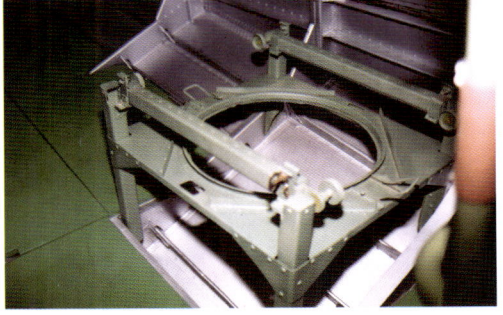

Supermarine Walrus & Stranraer

Detail photos

Top: The mooring rope cable reel, with the folded anchor to the right. The back of the instrument panel can be seen behind.

Middle: The roof of the centre-fuselage which acts as the lower centre section, carrying the loads from the wings to the fuselage.

Bottom right: The folded anchor.

Bottom left: A view into the nose, similar to the picture on page 71. All HD874.
(JDK)

Detail photos
Walrus Engine

The engine and propeller of A2-4. Both sets of blades were drilled so that they could not be fitted the wrong way around, after several accidents in which the aircraft failed to reach flying speed – sometimes off a catapult shot!

(RMW)

Lower: *The carburettor air intake (left) and the exhaust flame traps on L2301.*

(JDK)

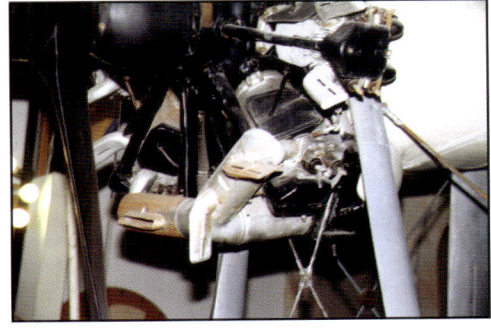

Supermarine Walrus & Stranraer 75

Detail photos

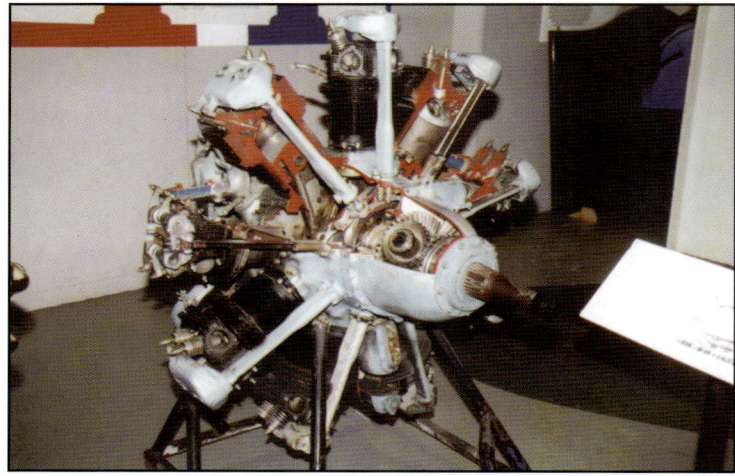

Top left: A different set of exhaust traps on A2-4. The "V" shaped tube gathered warm air for carburettor heating. Note the shields around the cylinders to direct cooling air. *Top right*: A sectioned Pegasus engine at the Fleet Air Arm Museum. A popular and reliable engine, used in the Swordfish as well as the Walrus and Stranraer. *Bottom*: The Pegasus on L2302, with the pointed spinner fitted, and many minor differences to the Pegasus fitted to A2-4. (All JDK)

Detail photos

The engine nacelle and support struts. Note the two fold-down footsteps fitted on the starboard forward strut on A2-4, and the single step (folded out) on L2301. Bottom left shows the two steps on L2301 folded out for use, and the two lower photos show the overall configuration and details of this area.
(All JDK)

Detail photos

Two shots of the nacelle of HD874, the right picture clearly illustrating the asymmetric strut arrangement. HD874 does not have the streamline fairings fitted around the struts, consequently the folded up steps are visible.
Bottom:
A vent on the side of the nacelle on L2301.

(All JDK)

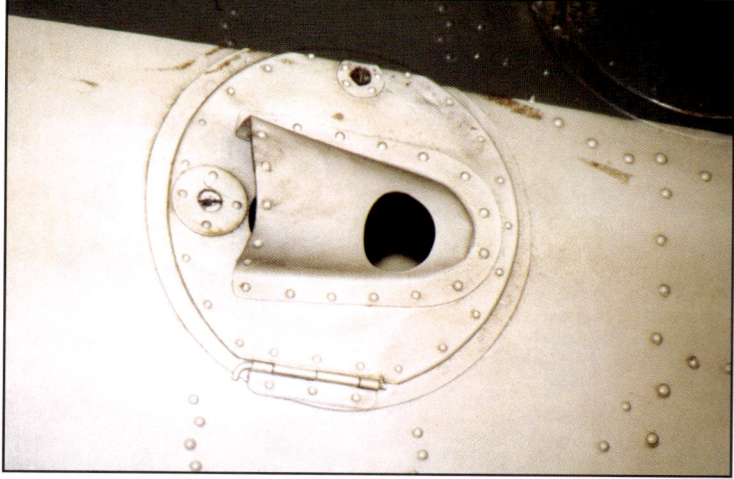

Detail photos

WALRUS
Floats & Undercarriage

This hard-used Walrus Mk.I being hoisted back aboard ship shows a good deal of otherwise unseen detail. Two canvas sea-anchors are still deployed, hanging below the fuselage. Many of the access panels and inspection ports are visible as is the outline of the folding flaps on the lower wings. Although the camouflage scheme is extremely worn and effectively indecipherable, two SEAC stars and bars can be discerned: one on the fuselage, the other on the port wing. Unusually, sealant has been needed on the hull joints to prevent water ingress. (FAAM) The wing float details. The production Walrus' float was deeper than the fatter and more flattened Sea Otter floats, and apparently larger than the prototype Seagull V.
(All JDK)

Supermarine Walrus & Stranraer

Detail photos

Details of the combined water-rudder and tail wheel as originally fitted, here on A2-4 (Top right) and (middle) on L2301. Apart from the water-rudder shape, this was essentially a tailskid with the tiny all-metal tail wheel inserted designed to stop damage to carrier decks. Most airfields were grass when the Walrus entered service, so a skid was a sensible option, and acted as a useful brake on landing on land. Top left is a rare example of the interim design, the rubber-tyre tail wheel / water rudder in Dick Melton's extensive collection of Walrus equipment. Bottom: A rear view of HD874's starboard float. The inspection hatches, tiedown loop and latch on the rear of the float are all visible.

(All JDK)

Detail photos

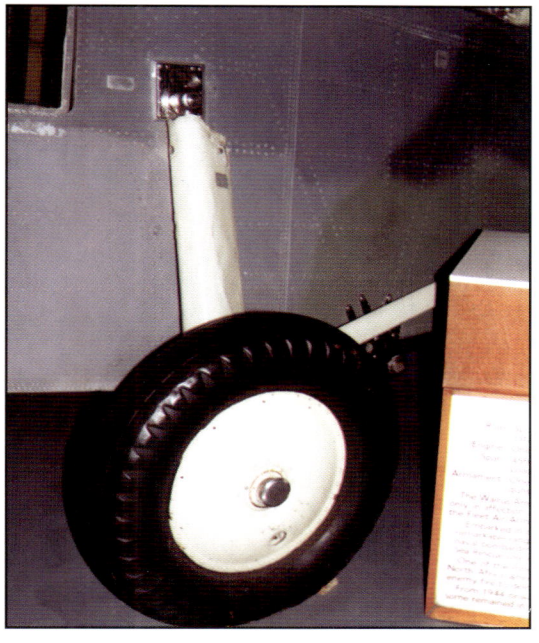

Clockwise from top left: HD874 has the later 'Sea Otter' style tail wheel, without any concession to a water rudder housing, found to be unnecessary. The main wheels on L2301, G-RNLI and HD874 respectively, all showing often-overlooked aspects of this configuration – particularly the small stub which locks into the fuselage side from the main leg. (All JDK)

Supermarine Walrus & Stranraer

Detail photos

The main leg of HD874, without the normally-fitted streamlined fairing, shows details of the oleo and the fuselage clip clearly. (Both JDK) Lower: An unidentified Walrus operating off HHS Shah in the far east. A very small white 'E' outlined in black can be seen on the original print, just below the oil-cooler intake. (FAAM)

Detail photos
STRANRAER
Fuselage

Above: Although often seen before, this shot of a RAF Stranraer of 240 Sqn gives a good idea of what an impression these big flying boats must have made. *(IWM)* *Below:* The sole surviving Supermarine Stranraer, Canadian built 920 CF-BXO has a number of significant differences to a service machine, particularly the engines, having been replaced with Wright R-1820 Cyclones with three blade Hamilton Standard propellers, but nevertheless it does get admiring glances from the RAF Museum's visitors.

(JDK)

Supermarine Walrus & Stranraer 83

Detail photos

Top:
The port side of 920.
(Mark Ansell)

Middle:
One of a sequence of pictures of Stranraer 923 being unloaded from a rail car used for transport in Canada. This view gives a clear outline of the hull shape.
(Shearwater)

Bottom:
The middle gunner's hatch in 920.
(JDK/RMW)

Detail photos

The rear hull of the Stranraer. It is deceptively more complex in shape than it seems at first glance.
(All JDK/RMW)

Detail photos

Top:
The rear beaching trolley.

Middle:
The centre section and beaching gear attachment.

Bottom right:
The beaching gear. The W.W.I Belfast Truss hangars at Hendon are not quite high enough to take the Stranraer on its gear, so the wheels have been removed to lower the aircraft a critical couple of feet.

Bottom left:
An overall view of the aircraft with the crew door open.

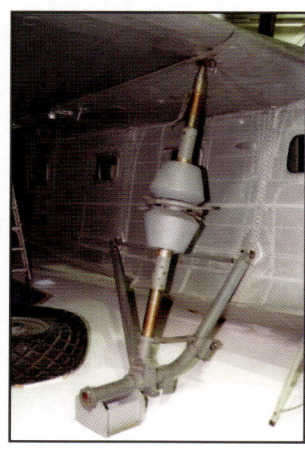

86 *Supermarine Walrus & Stranraer*

Detail photos

Top:
Another view of the starboard beaching gear. Gear varied, and this set is not typical of RAF units, and many Canadian units were also of a different type.

Middle & Bottom:
The crew entry door closed and open. The larger double hatch was inserted into CF-BXO /922 when it was converted to civil use, though the smaller inserted door is the same as in the military aircraft. There was an additional window forward of the door on military Stranraers, missing here.
(JDK/RMW)

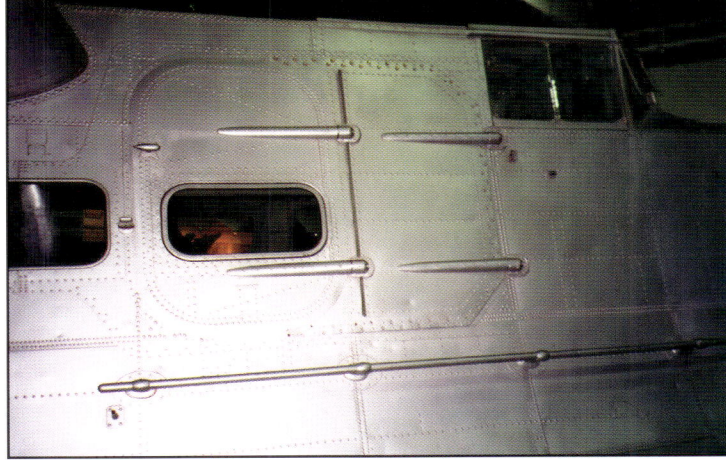

Supermarine Walrus & Stranraer **87**

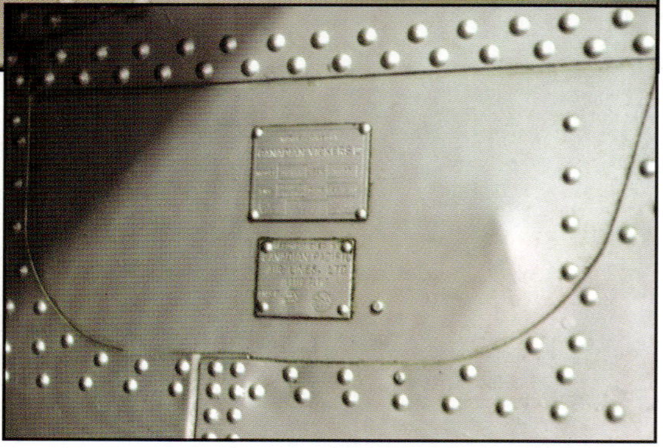

Detail photos

Top: The bow. Note the extreme curve of the flare to the spray-suppressing chine, and the foot rail around the nose above the waterline.
Middle right: The constructors' plate below the wing on the starboard side.
Middle left: The step, seen from the rear. Although the layout is similar, the Stranraer has a good number of curves compared to the Walrus' boxy construction. *Bottom*: The port wing root. Note the forward and aft hinged hatches. (JDK/RMW)

Detail photos

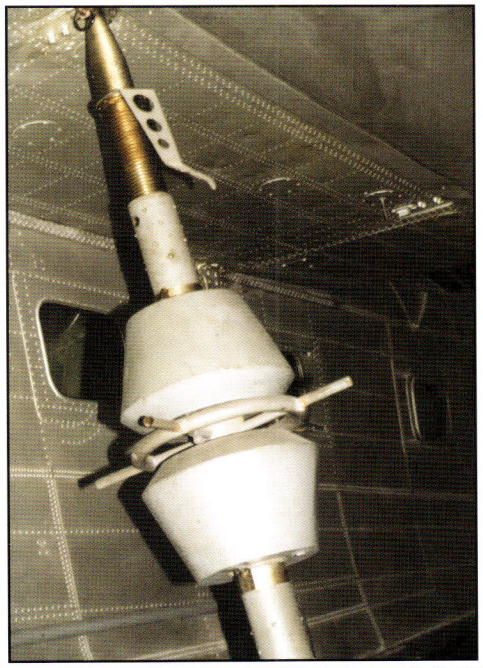

Above:
Details of the beaching gear. Although the actual equipment may vary, the mountings were always the same.

Left & Below:
The centre section and wing stubs from aft. This area was deliberately left clear so that it could be used as a load carriage area, as on the Scapa, but it seems to have been rarely utilised.

(JDK/RMW)

Detail photos

Top: From the same sequence as the pictures on page 84, 95 and 98, this shot shows the upper centre section being lowered onto 923. The waist gunner's windscreen can be seen, as well as its actuating mechanism, and the anti-corrosion treatment and staining on the hull below the waterline are also noteworthy.

A large amount of detail may be made out in this crisp picture. (Shearwater) *Middle*: The direction finding loop fairing on 920 (RMW) *Bottom*: A front three-quarter view giving a good overall idea of the size of the aircraft. (JDK)

Detail photos

Top:
One fuselage window, showing the hinge structure.

Middle:
The nose with the bomb-aimer's hatch and, above, the mooring bollards.
(*JDK/RMW*)

Bottom:
A picture of 920 / CF-BXO early on in civilian career before being re-engined.
(*CanAv*)

Detail photos
STRANRAER Wings

Top:
Stranraer 949 displays its RCAF roundels and fin flash as well as the wear and tear flying boat operations engender. (Shearwater)

Above: Early four-blade wooden prop shown here in a photo from a private album. (Shearwater).

Above Right: The engines and nacelles on 920. The nacelles are the same as service Stranraers, but only civil machines were fitted with the Wright engines. (JDK)

Detail photos

Top left:
920 has one ladder left erected as on display, although several positions were possible and they were normally removed before flight.

Top right:
The configuration of the outer starboard struts and aileron control seen from aft.

Middle:
The fuselage windows.

Bottom:
The port float and rigging.

(RMW)

Supermarine Walrus & Stranraer

Detail photos

***Top left**:*
Wing drain tube.

***Top right**:*
Wing float showing its single step classic shape. Internally it was divided into 4 separate compartments, to preserve buoyancy in case of damage; but as wing floats were often lost in their entirety in rough seas, with the result that the aircraft could not take off again, this was a minor achievement.

***Right**:*
A good view along the wing, with details of the two bay structure, ailerons and fabric surfaces.

(JDK/RMW)

94   Supermarine Walrus & Stranraer

Detail photos

Top left:
The port inner bay of 920 with the double flying wires clearly visible.

Top left:
The wingtip light.

Above:
The landing wire mounting by one wing strut.
(JDK/RMW)

Bottom:
Lowering the centre section onto 923.
(Shearwater)

Detail photos

Four views of the nacelle details of 920, as preserved. Engines, props and cowlings are all post-war modifications, but the nacelle struts, wing and fuel tanks are unchanged.

(JDK/RMW)

Detail photos
STRANRAER Tail

Three views of the Stranraer's tail, with a wartime view of the first Canadian-built Stranraer, 907 in the middle (Shearwater).
There was a noticeable gap between the horizontal tailplane and the fuselage.

(JDK/RMW)

Detail photos

Top left: The asymmetric leading edge of the elevators is well shown here. *Right*: The fin and rudder from aft, with the rear gunner's position in the foreground. *Bottom left*: The trim tab actuator on the port rudder from below. (All JDK / RMW) *Bottom right*: The tail being offered up to Stranraer 923. This clearly shows how it was a complete unit in its own right. (Shearwater)

Detail photos

STRANRAER Cockpit

Unfortunately, the interior of 920 is gutted, thanks to theft while in open store in Canada, so there is no instrument panel and almost no internal fittings left. The cockpit glazing of Stranraer 920 clearly shows a family resemblance to the Walrus, although much larger. The view from the pilot's seat (centre) shows how substantial the structure is.

(JDK/RMW)

Detail photos

Top left: Details of the control column base and rudder pedals. Right: Another private photo, illustrating the details of the scarff ring and blanking hatch unusually fitted beneath it in the amidships position, as well as the access hatch forward. The airman seems to be wearing the wrong outfit for jumping into the water! (Shearwater) Right bottom: The co-pilot's seat back support swung into position. The seat is long gone. Bottom left: The pilot's seat from the bow compartment. Note that the control runs are led up to the roof behind the cockpit. Opposite page: Details of the cockpit and pilot's seat. The standard seat raising lever, seen on many aircraft of the period, can be seen in the photo bottom right. (All JDK / RMW)

Detail photos

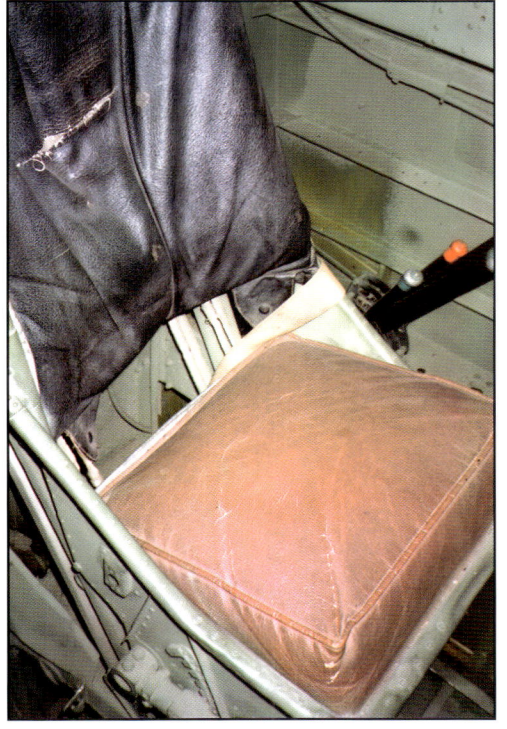

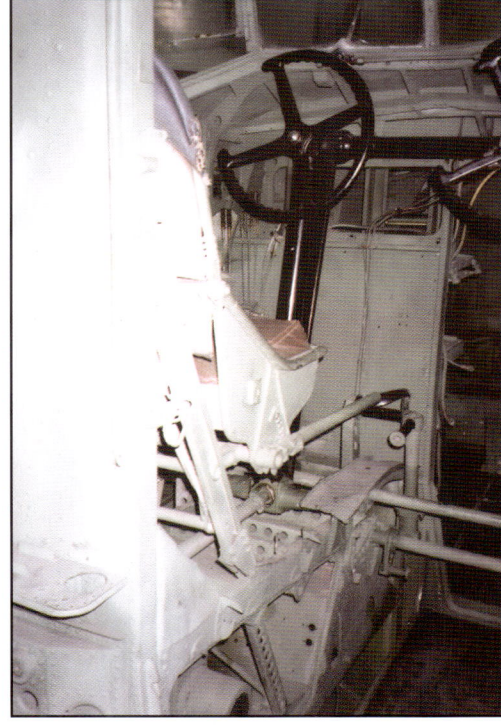

Detail photos
STRANRAER
Interior

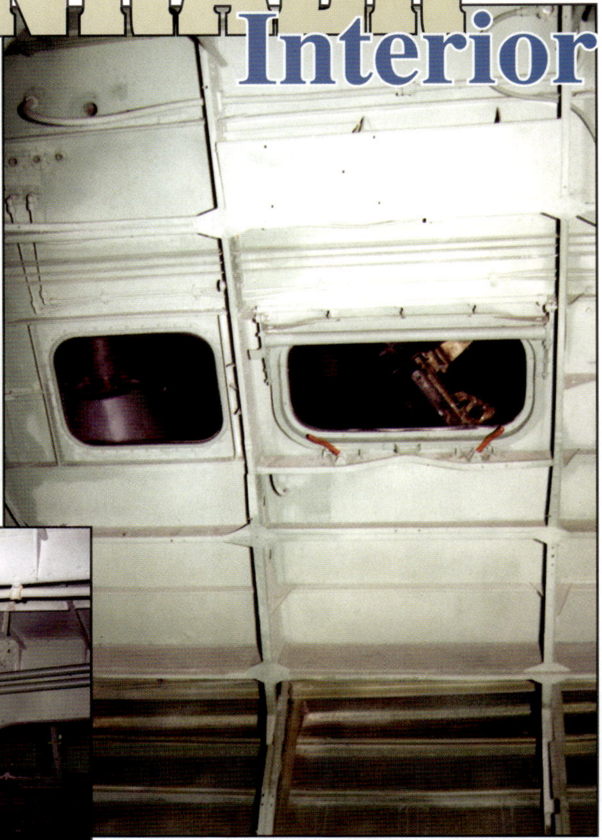

Top left: Looking in and aft from the crew entry door. *Top right*: The port midships compartment wall, showing the frame and stringer construction, and details of the hatches. *Middle*: The view forward from the compartment aft of the cockpit on the port side. The control runs were routed in the cabin roof to avoid submersion in the bilges and attendant problems. *Bottom*: Looking forward in the midships compartment at the starboard side.

(All JDK / RMW)

Detail photos

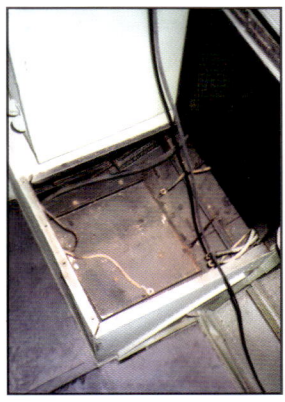

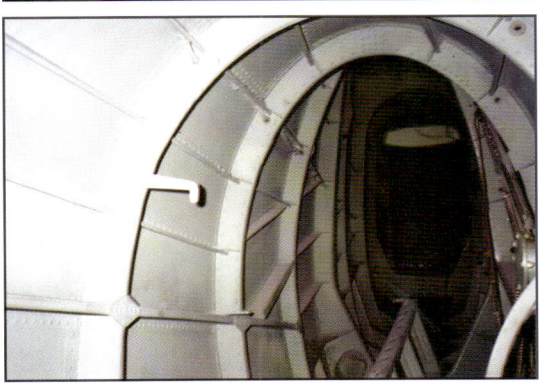

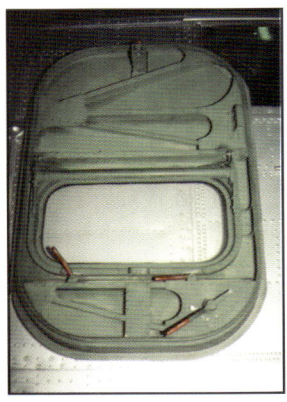

Left: The bow interior, showing internal details of the bomb-aimer's hatch, and the sliding bow hatch above for the bow gunner's use and mooring. All equipment fitted here is, sadly, long gone. *Top*: Access to the bilges. *Bottom right*: The crew door from below, showing its complex construction. *Bottom left*: The interior of the rear fuselage, and walkway to the tail gunner's position.

Detail photos

 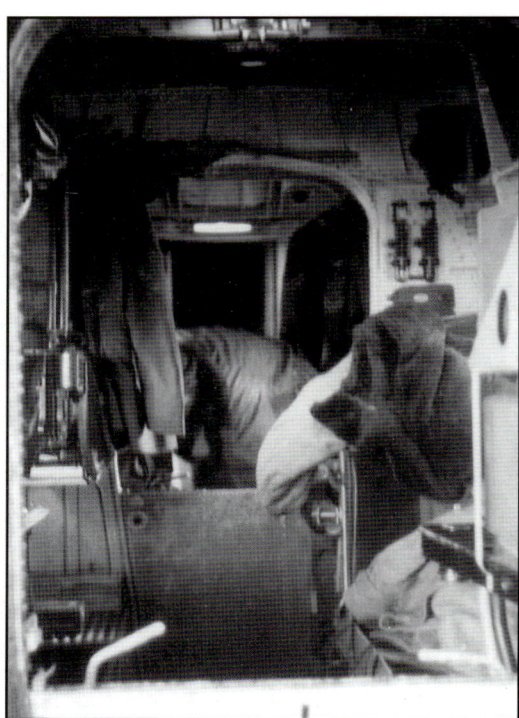

Clockwise from top left and right: Looking aft from the cockpit, in 920 (JDK) and a poor but very rare wartime interior photo providing a contrast in clutter. A host of details can be made out: the half doors fitted in the bulkheads to divide the fuselage into watertight sections; the two corporals' jackets hanging up, with a coat in the foreground; the galley sink on the left and an airman bending over; the radios and bench to the right foreground. (Shearwater) **Below right**: The centre gunner's hatch lowered and stowed. **Bottom left**: The racks forward of the instrument panel in the nose. **Opposite page, top left**: Another view of the rear fuselage with control runs on the right (port) and RAF Museum ladders on the left! Top right: Looking forward from the rear compartment through the bulkheads. **Below**: Looking into the rear fuselage through the rear gunner's hatch. (All JDK/RMW)

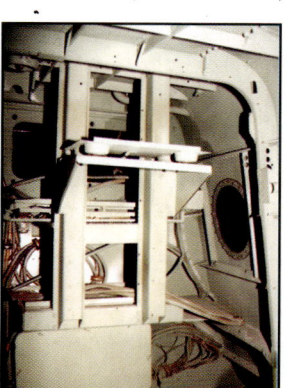 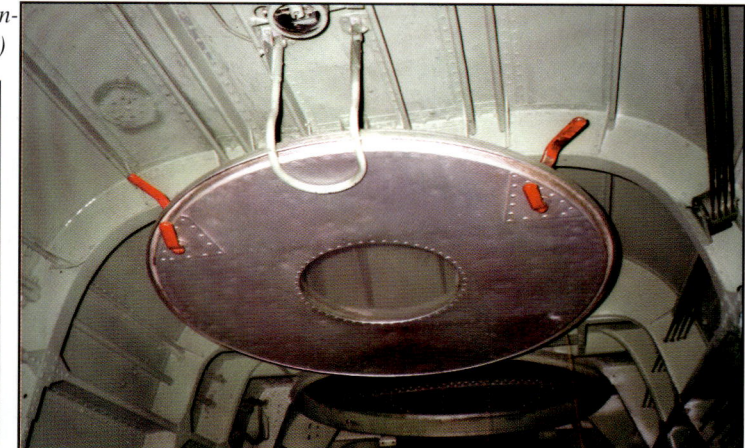

104 *Supermarine Walrus & Stranraer*

Detail photos

Supermarine Walrus & Stranraer 105

Colour profiles

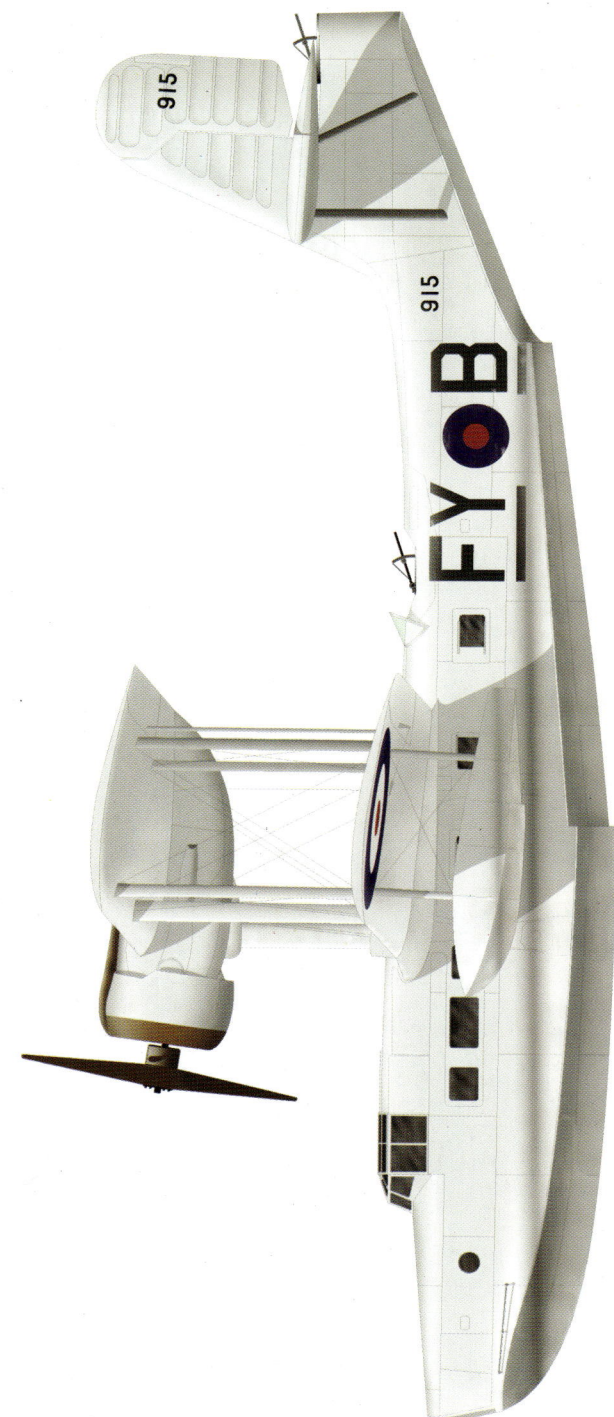

Stranraer 915 FY-B, 4 (BR) Sqn RCAF, RCAF Station Ucluelet, Vancouver Island, British Columbia. Seen in overall aluminium finish with type B roundel on the hull. Note the wooden four bladed propeller comprising two two-bladed units.

Colour profiles

Stranraer 937. 9 (BR) Sqn RCAF, RCAF Station Bella Bella, British Columbia, 1942-43. Seen in four colour counter shading. Lower surfaces are in sky. No codes carried at this time. This aircraft was seen in photographs with all guns mounted - unusual on most Stranraer operations.

Colour profiles

Stranraer 952 MX-C. 120 (BR) Sqn, RCAF Station Coal Harbour, 1942. Another west-coast based Stranraer, MX-C is seen in overall aluminium.

Colour profiles

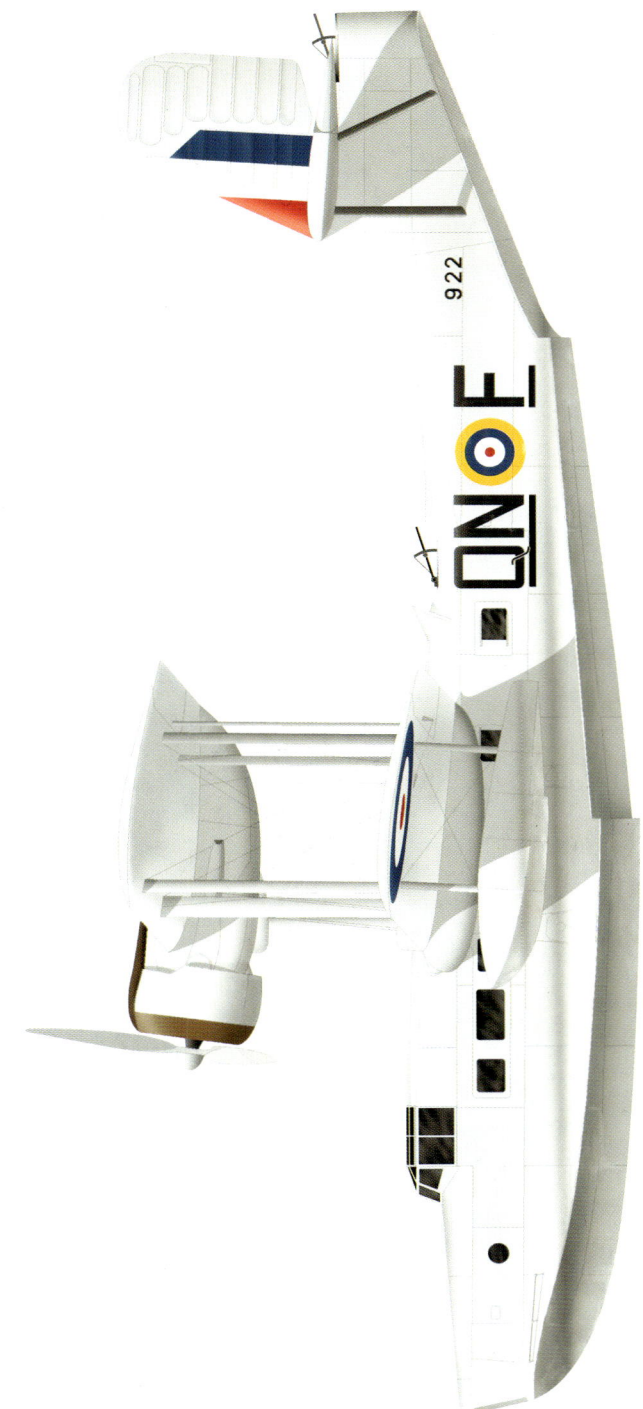

Stranraer 922. An aircraft of 5 (BR) Sqn RCAF, 922 carries the rarely illustrated long range fuel tanks inboard on the lower wing.

Colour profiles

Above:
Three stages in the life of sole complete surviving Stranraer 920 / CF-BXO. CF-BXO ca.1950. The "Alaska Queen" was one of two Stranraers that were given the more powerful engines in the postwar period, as illustrated. She is in overall aluminium with black and yellow trim.

Below:
Stranraer CF-BXO in it's next incarnation, with red over aluminium, as an aircraft of "Pacific Western", and as seen taking off from a special gear from the runway at Richmond, BC during June 1968.

Colour profiles

Stranraer 920 Hendon. The former CF-BXO as displayed since the 1970s at the RAF Museum, Hendon. She carries the markings of 5 (BR) Sqn RCAF, but is missing her individual aircraft letter. Extensive research has failed to establish what letter 920 carried in her wartime career, so she remains bereft. Note that she still has the postwar engines, propellers and cowlings.

Stranraer CF-BYL, sister ship to CF-BXO, illustrates another, earlier Queen Charlotte Airlines scheme, chosen for high visibility. Queen Charlotte Airlines operated numerous Stranraers in the postwar period, receiving local names ending in "Queen". Black hull with white trim, aluminium wings and tailplane.

Supermarine Walrus & Stranraer **111**

Colour profiles

Stranraer K7295, BN-L. 240 Sqn RAF, based appropriately at Stranraer, Scotland July 1940 - April 1941. This is the aircraft the Matchbox kit offers, and shows a two colour pattern of sea grey and slate grey, with aluminium undersurfaces.

Colour profiles

Stranraer RS-F. Another Coal Harbour based Stranraer, seen in 1942 wearing the often overlooked four-colour shadow shading pattern. Serial not known.

Colour profiles

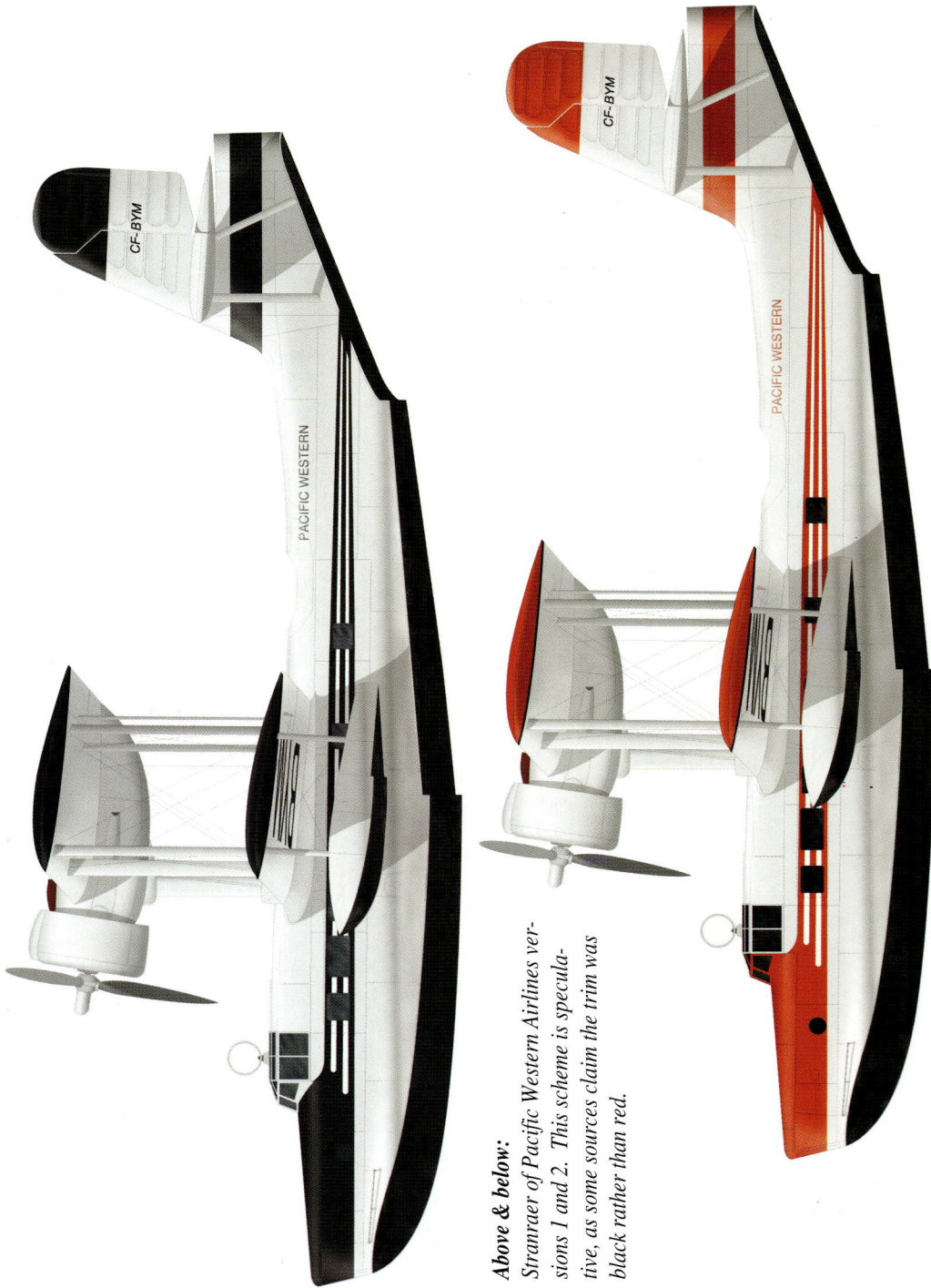

Above & below:
Stranraer of Pacific Western Airlines versions 1 and 2. This scheme is speculative, as some sources claim the trim was black rather than red.

Colour profiles

Walrus Mk. I L2190. 712 Sqn 1936-39. Overall aluminium finish and carrying either the blue band of HMS Cornwall or the yellow of HMS Birmingham this aircraft has been attributed to both ships by various sources.

Colour profiles

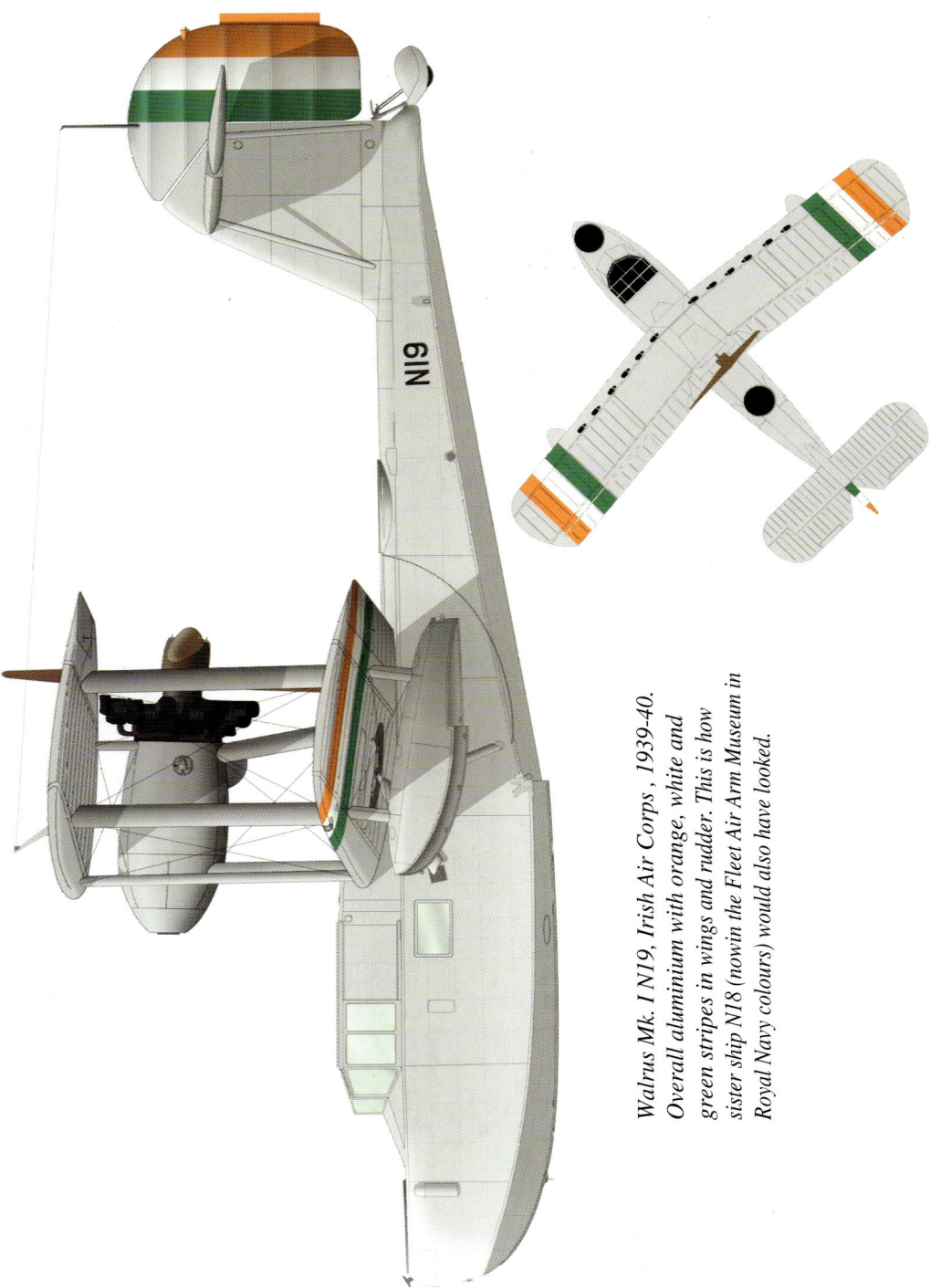

Walrus Mk. I N19, Irish Air Corps, 1939-40. Overall aluminium with orange, white and green stripes in wings and rudder. This is how sister ship N18 (now in the Fleet Air Arm Museum in Royal Navy colours) would also have looked.

Colour profiles

Walrus Mk. I L2236 of the training ship HMS Albatross. Two colour camouflage on the fuselage, shadow shading on the wings.

Colour profiles

Walrus Mk.I of the catapult flight aboard HMS Warspite. Four colour camouflage. Serial not confirmed.

Colour profiles

Walrus Mk. I, Operation Torch 1942. Dark Earth, Middle Stone, Azure Blue finish. British aircraft engaged in Operation Torch (the Anglo-American landings in North Africa) carried American markings to try and minimise the reaction from the Vichy French defenders.

Colour profiles

Walrus Mk. I X9559, flown by Leading Aircraftsman Ward, 2nd Lt Leyland and Lt Hunt. No. 700 Sqn FAA HMS Howe, and shore base RNAS Twatt, Dec 1942. An unusual application of a two colour scheme, particularly notable around the bow area.

Colour profiles

Wooden hulled air sea rescue Walrus Mk. II HD925 of 275 Sqn RAF. Shown in 2- colour camouflage, but this is somewhat speculative.

Supermarine Walrus & Stranraer **121**

Colour profiles

Record setting ASR Walrus Mk. I P5658 of 276 Sqn RAF. AQ-M carries unusual mission markings, each being a stylised lifebelt with the number of rescuees carried within, the maximum being seven. Four colour camouflage with light grey codes. Note the handrails along the hull sides, shorter on the starboard than on the port.

Colour profiles

Wooden hulled ASR Walrus Mk. II HD908 BA-D of 277 Sqn RAF, 1944-45. BA-D wears a four colour camouflage the exact pattern of which is uncertain.

Colour profiles

RAAF ASR Walrus Mk. I "Rescue Girl" (unknown serial) serving with 71 Wing in the Admiralty Islands, Sept 1944. Colours of the mermaid are unconfirmed. Note the primer painted front half of the engine nacelle.

Colour profiles

RAAF Walrus MkI HD874 is the RAAF Museum's example. Seen here in the colours it wore on departure to the Antarctic - originally in Royal Navy four colour scheme, it was (possibly) painted into an overall green scheme, with SEAC roundels. The roundels were retained when this overall yellow was applied, which then had the new postwar three colour roundels added as the last change, when it was actually in the Antarctic. We illustrate the penultimate scheme, a slight variation to its preserved configuration.

Supermarine Walrus & Stranraer **125**

Colour profiles

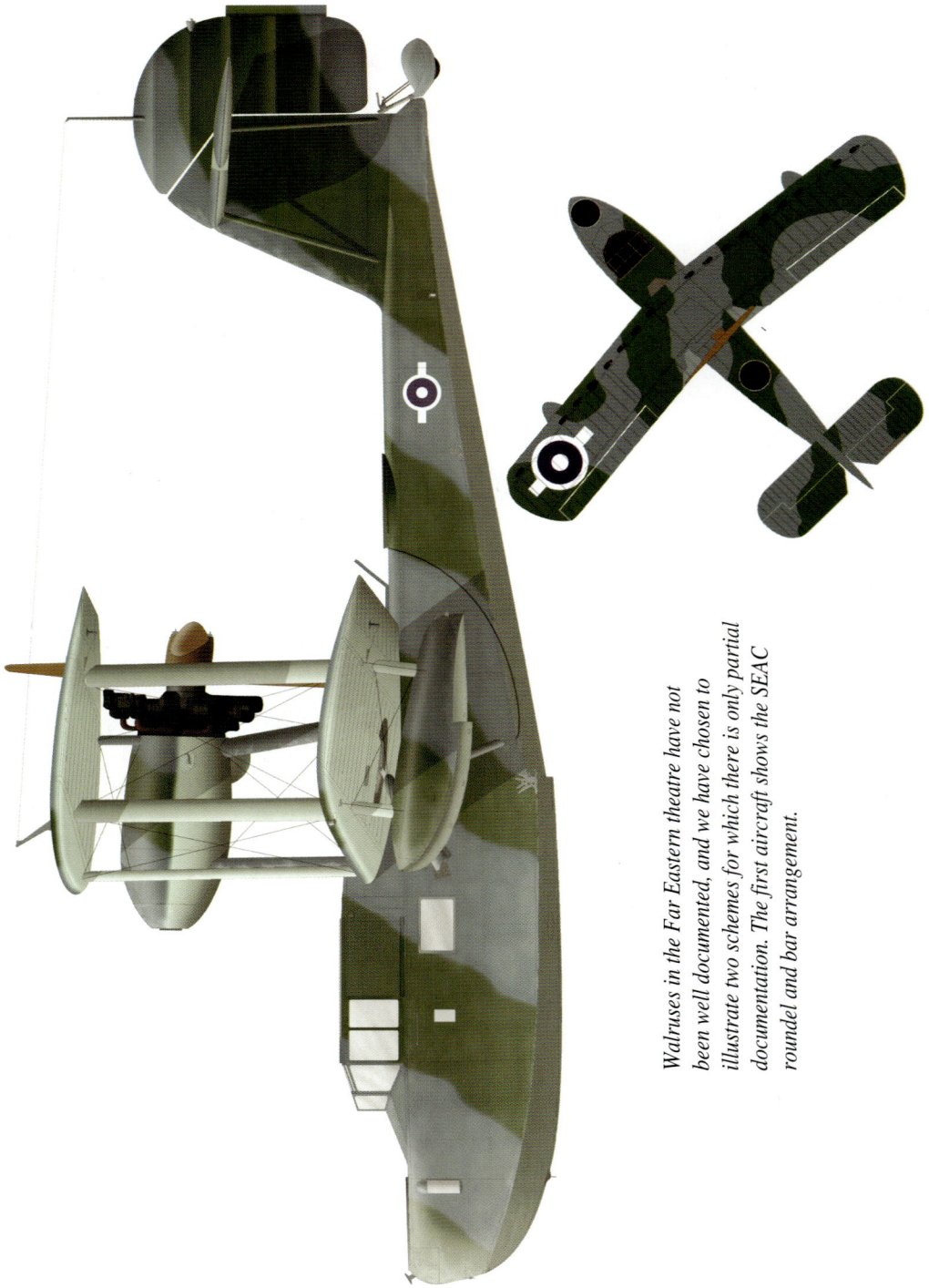

Walruses in the Far Eastern theatre have not been well documented, and we have chosen to illustrate two schemes for which there is only partial documentation. The first aircraft shows the SEAC roundel and bar arrangement.

Colour profiles

This machine has the white bars across the tail and wings, as well as small SEAC roundels. Serials and full details for both machines have not been confirmed.

Colour profiles

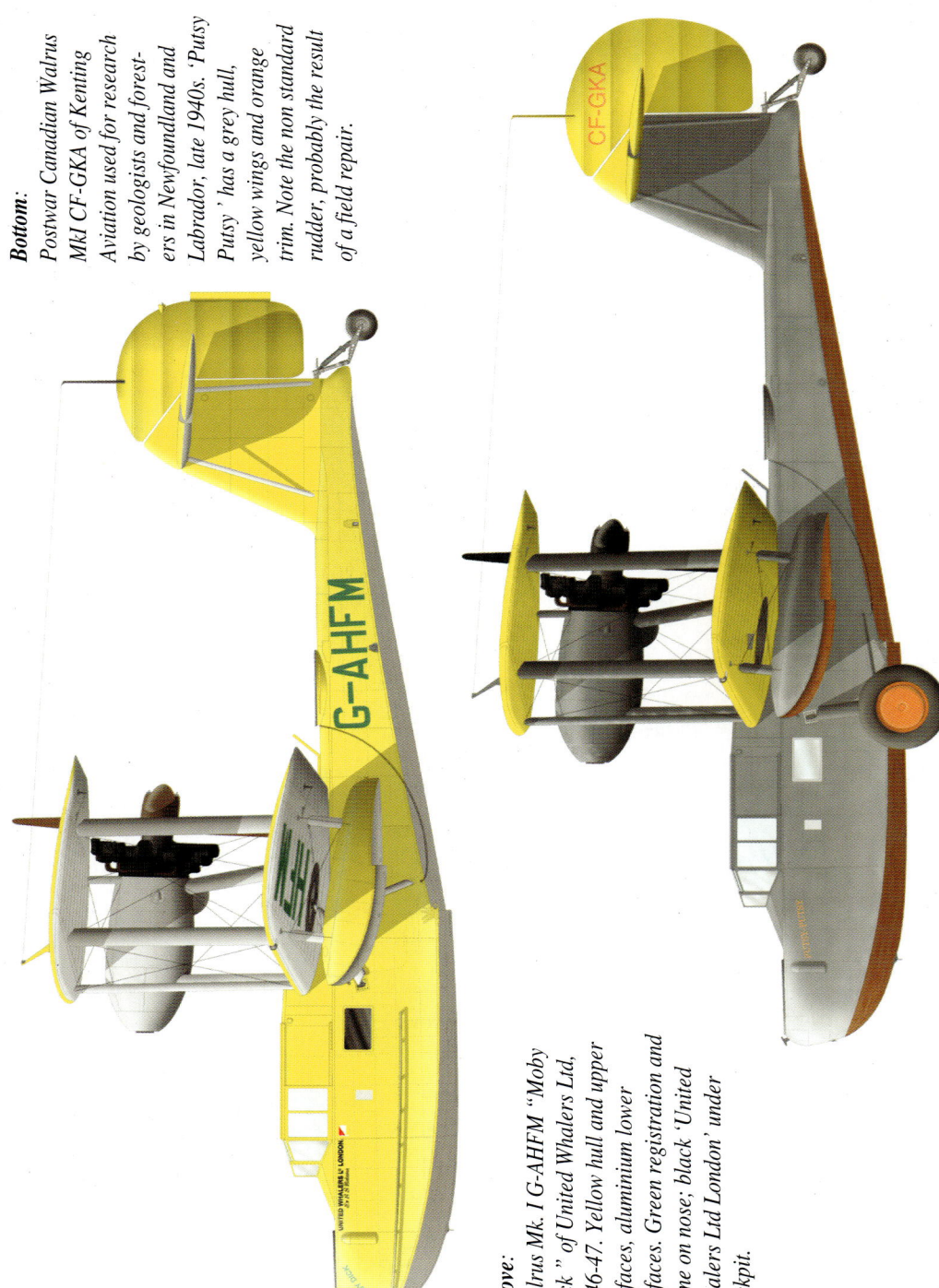

Bottom: Postwar Canadian Walrus MkI CF-GKA of Kenting Aviation used for research by geologists and foresters in Newfoundland and Labrador, late 1940s. 'Putsy' has a grey hull, yellow wings and orange trim. Note the non standard rudder, probably the result of a field repair.

Above: Walrus Mk. I G-AHFM "Moby Dick" of United Whalers Ltd, 1946-47. Yellow hull and upper surfaces, aluminium lower surfaces. Green registration and name on nose; black 'United Whalers Ltd London' under cockpit.

128   *Supermarine Walrus & Stranraer*